REREADING ROMANS
from THE PERSPECTIVE
of PAUL'S GOSPEL

REREADING ROMANS
from THE PERSPECTIVE
of PAUL'S GOSPEL

A Literary and Theological Commentary

Yung Suk Kim

RESOURCE *Publications* · Eugene, Oregon

REREADING ROMANS FROM THE PERSPECTIVE
OF PAUL'S GOSPEL
A Literary and Theological Commentary

Resource Publications
An Imprint of Wipf and Stock Publishers
199 W. 8th Ave., Suite 3
Eugene, OR 97401

www.wipfandstock.com

PAPERBACK ISBN: 978-1-5326-9309-0
HARDCOVER ISBN: 978-1-5326-9310-6
EBOOK ISBN: 978-1-5326-9311-3

Manufactured in the U.S.A.   04/18/19

Contents

Preface

PAUL DID NOT WRITE a systematic theology or specific church doctrines when he wrote Romans. His audience was Roman Christians and his last will was to preach the gospel to all, especially people in Spain. The question is: What kind of the gospel he wants to share with them? Traditionally, the letter has been read from the lens of "justification by faith," but the letter is not about an individual justification from the perspective of forensic salvation. We need to reread the letter with a renewed concept of the good news in the letter. The main question for Paul in the letter is how Gentiles can become children of God as well as how Jews may live faithfully in Christ. Indeed, the gospel is the grand theme of the letter, as he says he was "set apart for the gospel of God" (1:1). His apostleship is for this mission that he must proclaim the gospel of God. In this apostolic work, he follows Christ thoroughly. That is, he imitates Christ because of his faithful obedience to God. That is why Paul identifies himself as a slave of Christ (1:1), which means his obedient life to him. Paul thinks he is the last-day apostle who can bring Gentiles to Jerusalem. His job is not to destroy Judaism or Jerusalem Temple but to bring God's good news to all through Jesus Christ, especially through his faithfulness.

In sum, in Paul's gospel, God is the source of the good news, Jesus is the proclaimer of it, and Christians are those who share Jesus's faithfulness and follow his spirit. Paul is confident about this gospel as he says in 1:16: "For I am not ashamed of the gospel; it is the power of God for salvation to everyone who has faith, to the Jew first and also to the Greek."

In his gospel, faith does not overthrow the law (3:31). The problem is not the law per se but a zeal for the law. That is, all that is not done through faith is sin (14:22–23). The relation between faith and the law is a matter of priority (Rom 3–4). The law must be guided by faith and the grace of God. In his gospel, Rom 9–11 is also an important part of the gospel because, as he says in 1:16, the gospel is the power of God for salvation to everyone, including Jews. He rejects the claim that God abandoned his people (11:2). Even though they are unfaithful now, he believes that God will work out their salvation at an opportune time (11:25–32).

This book is not a typical, thoroughgoing commentary with verse by verse. It is a mixture of commentary and monograph with a thesis. It has a form of commentary in the way that it outlines the entire letter and comments on the entire text. The only difference is it goes with not verse by verse but with a literary unit by unit. This book has a form of a monograph in the sense that it has a thesis and the unified direction toward it, which is about the gospel. This mixture style of a book will be applied to my next book forthcoming: *Rereading Galatians from the Perspective of Paul's Gospel: A Literary and Theological Commentary* (Cascade, 2019).

With the above book format, Romans will be reorganized with a theme of the "good news" and will be commented critically and theologically. Rom 1:1–17 is considered a prologue to the entire letter. Here, Paul talks about why he writes a letter and what he tries to achieve with it. He states a few times that he is eager to share the gospel with all, especially the so-called barbarians and the foolish. Then, Rom 1:18–11:36 deals with the gospel of faith that does not reject the law or Israel. Within this section, the following divisions are made: 1:18–3:20 The Problem of Unfaithfulness; 3:21–4:25 Righteousness through Christ's Faithfulness; 5:1–21 New Life through Christ's Act of Righteousness; 6:1–7:25 Maintenance of New Life: Dying to Sin and Dying to the Law; 8:1–39 New Life in the Spirit; 9:1–29 The Dilemma of Israel in the Gospel of God; 9:30–10:21 Righteousness for Jew and Gentile through Faithfulness; 11:1–36 The Mystery of Salvation of Israel. Then Rom 12:1–15:13 deals with the gospel's power of transformation to individuals and communities. Lastly, Rom 15:14–16:27 deals with concluding matters of the gospel.

Introduction

TRADITIONALLY, ROMANS HAS BEEN interpreted from a forensic salvation perspective, and Paul's gospel has been understood through the doctrine of "justification by faith." In this doctrine, justification is understood as an individual justification. That is, sinners in a court are declared righteous by the judge, who is God, because of Jesus's vicarious death. In this view, Jesus completed the salvific work by dying on the cross on behalf of sinners, and sins were dealt with properly by his death. In this reading, Jesus's death is required for an individual justification or for the atonement of sinners. For example, Christ delivered sinners from the grip of the devil by paying the ransom (ransom theory). He was punished and died instead of sinners (penal-substitution theory). His sacrifice was a propitiation to allay God's wrath (propitiation theory). His death was a cost needing to restore a broken relationship between God and humanity (expiation theory). His sinless sacrifice was necessary to satisfy God's high moral standard that sinners would not be forgiven without such a perfect price (satisfaction theory). In all the above atonement theories, Jesus's death is necessary to deal with sins, and what believers need is faith in him. If they believe and accept his salvific death, their sins are cleansed or dealt with. The result is each person is considered righteous ("imputed righteousness") or given a righteousness ("imparted righteousness").[1]

Likewise, interpreters have read Rom 1:16 and 3:22 in view of the doctrine of "justification by faith" and translated *pistis christou* as an objective genitive: "faith in Christ." Most English Bibles, including the New Revised Standard Version (NRSV) and New International Version (NIV),

---

1. "Imputed righteousness" is seen in Luther's interpretation. *Luther's Works Vol. 12,* pages 366—367. "Imparted or infused righteousness" is seen in Augustine's work. See https://www.ccel.org/ccel/schaff/npnf105.xi.ii.html, Accessed March 10, 2019. Extract from Augustine's "Retractations," Book 2, Chapter 37, "De Spiritu Et Littera."

have this objective genitive translation. This translation serves the doctrine of "individual justification by faith" in that Christ completed the salvific work. But this objective genitive understanding of *pistis christou* is very problematic because we ignore the importance of Jesus's faithfulness and his moral sacrifice. Therefore, we need to reread Romans not only about *pistis christou* but about Paul's gospel as a whole. Traditionally, Paul's gospel has been understood as individualistic salvation and justification by faith. So much so the center of his gospel needed Christ's once and for all sacrifice to deal with sin. But Paul's gospel goes beyond that dimension. He wants to communicate with the Roman Christians that his gospel is not anti-law or anti-Israel and that it is faith-rooted good news that already began with Abraham. It is very important to reread Romans from the perspective of Paul's gospel and reevaluate his language of faith, justification, law, and Israel.

Paul's gospel features "the good news of God," "the good news of Jesus," and "the good news that Jesus's followers proclaim." Interpreters often do not see the importance of God's good news that is proclaimed by Jesus. Paul's gospel is not simply about justification by faith (as held by many evangelical scholars) but about God's power that is effective to all who participate in Christ's faithfulness.

From the outset, it would be helpful to enumerate the special features of this book. First, traditionally, Rom 1–8 has been considered the center of the gospel. That is "justification by faith," not by the law. But this old view does not gain ground these days, as Stendahl already began to tackle it in the early 1980s. Indeed, Rom 9–11 is an important, necessary part of the gospel because, as Paul states in 1:16 ("to the Jew first and also to the Greek"), the gospel would be incomplete without the participation of Jews. More than that, Rom 12–16 is also an important part of the gospel because the gospel is the power of God for salvation. In these chapters, Paul talks about the power of the gospel effective to people and communities.

Second, usually, Rom 12–16 is treated as ethical exhortations or the Christian ethical part. The idea here is that theology or gospel in Rom 1–8 is separated from ethics in Rom 12–16. In other words, the former is understood as an indicative mood ("You are a Christian or saved") and the latter is an imperative mood ("Therefore, show good works"). The implication here is clear in that justification is only by faith, not by works. In this view, while the ethical part is important to Christian identity, it is not decisive to justification. But Paul never separates between faith and works as if works are not important to justification. In his thinking, the gospel is the power of God for salvation (1:16). Therefore, if there is no power of God in Christian lives or in the communities, there is no gospel. That is why this book reads Rom 12–16 as "the gospel's power of transformation."

Third, a long-debated issue of *pistis christou* ("faith of Christ") may be resolved in this book because it is understood well as Christ's faithfulness through which God's righteousness has been manifested and the followers of Jesus have to base their faith in him. They have to participate in his life and death. God also justifies those who share Jesus's faithfulness (3:26). This above view of *pistis christou* makes better sense than that of E. P. Sanders or N. T. Wright, who does not address the importance of Christ's faithfulness in God's gospel. But Richard Hays and Luke T. Johnson are with me as they see the significance of Jesus's faithful work to God.

Fourth, faith has been the basis for the right relationship with God from Abraham to Jesus and afterward. Faith means faithfulness to God, trusting him, believing in his promise, and submitting to his will. In Paul's view, faith came with Abraham before the law was given. Jesus was also faithful to God and disclosed his righteousness. All those who follow Jesus must have the faithfulness of Jesus.

Fifth, Jesus's death also can be understood differently in Romans. Jesus's crucifixion is not necessary for the forgiveness of sins or for meeting the needs of the traditional atonement theories such as penal-substitution theory or satisfaction theory. His death represents a tragic yet costly love of people when he was faithful to the God of justice and peace. Likewise, *hilasterion* in Rom 3:25 may be understood differently as "a new locus of reconciliation" rather than the usual translation of "a sacrifice of atonement" in the NRSV and NIV. This book's point seems unique and makes sense to some feminist or womanist readers who do not subscribe to the traditional atonement theories.

Sixth, God did not reject his people, Israel, and their salvation depends on God's mercy and his sovereignty. According to Paul, the problem for Jews is twofold: (1) They have "a zeal for God" which is unenlightened; (2) they refuse to accept Jesus as the Messiah. The New Perspective on Paul shed new light on our understanding of Paul. In fact, Paul's gospel is one and the same for Jews and Gentiles since faith is the common ground on which all are justified, as Rom 3:30 says: "Since God is one; and he will justify the circumcised on the ground of faith and the uncircumcised through that same faith."

Section I

1:1–17

Prologue to Romans

1:1–17 IS A PROLOGUE to, and synopsis, of Romans. Here Paul insinuates why he writes Romans and what he will discuss. On the one hand, he writes to defend "the gospel of faith" for all (1:16–17), and on the other hand, he wants to pave the way for a visit to Rome so that he could go to Spain in his mission trip through their support (1:11–15; c.f., 15:22–29).[1] He clarifies the meaning of "the gospel of faith" throughout Rom 1–11. It means that the gospel or good news is received by faith. Otherwise, faith does not overthrow the law or reject Israel, as he says clearly about this: "Do we then overthrow the law by this faith? By no means! On the contrary, we uphold the law" (3:31). Indeed, "the law is holy, and the commandment is holy and just and good" (7:12). The problem is not the law *per se* but those who misunderstand the law or misuse it. He states well about this in 10:1–3: "Brothers and sisters, my heart's desire and prayer to God for them is that they may be saved. I can testify that they have a zeal for God, but it is not enlightened. For, being ignorant of the righteousness that comes from God, and seeking to establish their own, they have not submitted to God's righteousness." Paul argues that what comes first is not the law but the promise of God. Faith is to believe this promise of God, trusting him and submitting to God's righteousness (10:3). Faith precedes and informs the law. This means the latter is kept carefully through the lens of faith, which is to honor God's will and to submit to his righteousness. Faith is

1. Krister Stendahl's small book on Romans emphasizes the importance of Paul's final mission "within the total plan of God." Krister Stendahl, *Final Account*, 12.

4

needed all the time and people have to live by it in all circumstances. So Paul quotes from Hab 2:4: "The righteous one will live by faith." His point is that God's righteousness—his love and mercy—will be freely available and effective to all who have faith. He wants to share this gospel of faith with all, including people in Spain.

"The gospel of faith" begins with God, who is the source of life and the origin of the good news. Thus Paul makes clear that he is a "slave of Christ Jesus, an apostle called and set apart for the gospel of God" (1:1). As an apostle, his job is to proclaim "the good news of God" (εὐαγγέλιον θεοῦ, *euangelion theou*), not his own gospel apart from God or Jesus. "Being set apart" (ἀφωρισμένος, *aphorismenos*) in 1:1 implies that his mission is prophetic. Like a prophet, he is called to do a special task for God, which is none other than proclaiming "the gospel of God."[2] More than that, his work also involves a priestly service of the gospel of God, as he says in 15:16: "a minister of Christ Jesus to the Gentiles in the priestly service of the gospel of God, so that the offering of the Gentiles may be acceptable, sanctified by the Holy Spirit."

In 1:2, Paul talks about the origin of the gospel of God: "which he [God] promised beforehand through his prophets in the holy scriptures." This implies that the gospel of God traces back to the story of the Old Testament in which prophets and various agents of God have worked for God. The gospel of God is not a new concept but it has been understood and proclaimed throughout the time of the Old Testament. But it has not been very successful because of human disobedience to God. Therefore, in 1:3–4, the Son of God is introduced; Jesus was faithful to God and proclaimed God's good news at the risk of his life. He disclosed God's righteousness through faithfulness. Thus now the gospel of God concerns his Son Jesus: "The gospel [of God] concerning his Son, who was descended from David according to the flesh and was declared to be Son of God with power according to the spirit of holiness by resurrection from the dead, Jesus Christ our Lord."[3] Paul distinguishes between Jesus "who was descended from David according to the flesh" (1:3) and Christ the declared (ὁρισθέντος, *horisthentos*) Son of God (1:4). As a declared son of God, he proclaimed the good news of God to reveal God's righteousness (c.f., 3:22). What Jesus

2. "The gospel of God" also appears in the following: Rom 15:16; 2 Cor 11:7; 1 Thess 2:2, 8, 9; Mark 1:14; 1 Pet 4:17.

3. In the Gospel stories, Jesus is adopted as Son of God at his baptism (Mark 1:9–11; Luke 3:21–22; Matt 3:13–17). After this, he proclaims the good news of God and does the work of God.

did for God constitutes "the gospel of Christ" through which Paul serves or worships (λατρεύω, *latreuo*) God.[4] This idea is conveyed in Rom 1:9: "For God, whom I worship with my spirit by announcing the gospel of his Son, is my witness that without ceasing I remember you always in my prayers."

Through Jesus, Roman Christians have received grace and apostleship (1:5). They are all called to serve God through Jesus. Likewise, Paul is deeply committed to sharing this good news of God through Jesus, expressing his desire to proclaim the gospel "to Greeks and to barbarians, both to the wise and to the foolish" (1:14–15). Then, he summarizes the gospel: "For I am not ashamed of the gospel; it is the power of God for salvation to everyone who has faith, to the Jew first and also to the Greek. For in it the righteousness of God is revealed from faith to faith; as it is written, 'The one who is righteous will live by faith'" (1:16–17). The gospel is not merely a message about God but "the power of God for salvation to everyone who has faith, to the Jew first, and also to the Greek" (1:16). The gospel as the power of God comes through faith, which means to submit to God. In this gospel, there is no discrimination against people on the basis of race, religion, class, or gender. All people can join the children of God through faith.

As we see above, important themes of Romans are introduced in 1:1–17: "the gospel" (εὐαγγέλιον, *euangelion*), "faith" (πίστις, *pistis*), and "righteousness" (δικαιοσύνη, *dikaiosyne*). These themes are explored throughout the letter. For example, in 1:18–3:20, he talks about why God's righteousness was not a reality of people in everyday life. That is, here the problem is human unfaithfulness and suppression of the truth. In 3:21–4:25, he explores the basis of one's justification with God, which is through faith. In 5:1–21, he emphasizes Christ's act of righteousness, showing the example of Christ's faithfulness. Thus, the implication is Christians have to participate in his faithfulness. In 6:1–7:25, he goes deeper to explain what it means to live by faith. That is to die with Christ, which means dying to sin. In 8:1–39, he talks about a new life in the Spirit, which requires "to put to death the deeds of the body" by the Spirit (8:13). In 9–11, he deals with the dilemma of Israel in the gospel of God. In Rom 12:1–15:13, he defends and advocates the gospel's transformative power in the community and society. In 15:14–16:27, he concludes his gospel with concluding reflections.

---

4. "The gospel of Christ" appears in the following: 1 Cor 9:12; 2 Cor 9:13; Gal 1:7; Phil 1:27; 1 Thess 3:2.

Outline of 1:1–17

1:1–4 PAUL'S CALLING FOR THE GOSPEL OF GOD CONCERNING HIS SON

Slave Metaphor (1:1)

Paul's self-identification as a "slave (δοῦλος, *doulos*) of Christ Jesus" in 1:1 is hard to understand. The usual interpretation is to understand the slavery metaphor as a servant in the OT prophetic sense.[5] For example, some prophets are called the "slave of Yahweh" (Amos 3:7; Jer 7:25; Dan 9:6). From this perspective, "slave of Jesus" is construed as a servant or a prophet of Jesus. Paul thinks he is sent by Jesus and works for him. But this view seems to contradict his own view that he sees himself as the one who is called and sent by God, as Gal 1:15–16 says: "But when God, who had set me apart before I was born and called me through his grace, was pleased to reveal his Son to me, so that I might proclaim him among the Gentiles, I did not confer with any human being." Moreover, if Paul had meant to be a "servant of Jesus," he would have used διάκονός (*diakonos*), as a similar use is found in 13:4: "servant of God."

The other interpretive option is to read the slave metaphor from an anti-imperial, rhetorical perspective, as Jewett does. He reads "slave of Jesus" as a ministerial honorary title, compared to the slave of Caesar.[6] He argues that "slave of Jesus" is superior to "slave of Caesar." He observes as follows: "The proximity between 'slave of Caesar' and 'slave of Christ Jesus' sets an agenda pursued throughout the letter concerning *whose power is ultimate, whose gospel is efficacious, and whose program for global pacification and unification is finally viable*" (Italics for emphasis).[7] An imperial slave

---

5. Richard Longenecker, *Romans*, 50–52. See also James Dunn, *Romans 1–8*, 7–8.

6. Robert Jewett, *Romans*, 99–101. See also M. J. Brown, "Paul's Use of *doulos christou Iesou* in Romans 1:1," 723–37.

7. Jewett, *Romans*, 100–101.

feels honored because of his service to Caesar, but Paul is more honored because of his service to Christ whose power is ultimate, whose gospel is more efficacious, and whose program for global peace and unification is more viable than Caesar. Paul counters imperial propaganda of "security and peace." But in this interpretation, the weakness is the power of God's gospel is less emphasized. That is, Paul's gospel begins with God (as in "the gospel of God," in 1:1), not with Jesus. God is more powerful than Jesus, who revealed God's righteousness. The ultimate power is given to God (c.f., 1 Cor 15:28).[8] God is the owner of the church and Christ is its foundation. In fact, Paul's preferred term for the Christian community is "the church of God," not the church of Christ.[9] He worships (λατρεύω) God through Jesus (1:9).

The other interpretive option is to read the slave metaphor as a mode of solidarity with the slaves in and outside of the Roman church.[10] By calling himself a slave, he identifies with all slaves in the Roman church and comforts them with the message about Jesus, who was maimed and crucified due to injustices but was resurrected by God.

All the above options have merit but they are also limited. The slave metaphor in Rom 1:1 can be better interpreted as an obedient life focused on Christ's way of life.[11] That is, the slave metaphor reinforces Paul's willingness to follow Jesus. As Jesus was obedient to God, Paul is committed to following Jesus. Thus he wants to live in him and live by his faithfulness. Such an idea is well expressed in Gal 2:20: "And it is no longer I who live, but it is Christ who lives in me. And the life I now live in the flesh I live *by* (or *in*) *the faith of the Son of God* (ἐν πίστει ζῶ τῇ τοῦ υἱοῦ τοῦ θεοῦ), who loved me and gave himself for me." "Faith of the Son of God" must be a subjective genitive. That is, he is determined to live by (or in) the faithfulness of the Son of God. This above use of the slave metaphor appears throughout Paul's undisputed letters. See the following:

8. For Paul, Christ is a servant of God and yields to God on the last day (1 Cor 15:28). Not only God's power is ultimate, but the gospel's power comes from God (1:16).

9. "The church of God" appears in the following: 1 Cor 1:2; 10:32; 11:22; 15:9; Gal 1:3.

10. K. Edwin Bryant's dissertation on Romans highlights this aspect of slavery metaphor as a mode of Paul's solidarity with the slaves in Rome. He argues that the Messiah Jesus's exemplary life and sacrifice awaken the consciousness of slaves so that they may live with hopes in God, fighting Roman imperialism and the domination of power. See K. Edwin Bryant, *Paul and the Rise of the Slave*, 28–107.

11. See Joseph Fitzmyer, *Romans*, 231.

- In Rom 6:15–22 and 7:1–25, "slaves of sin" is contrasted with "slaves of righteousness." The former means to yield to sin, and the latter, to be committed to the work of righteousness.

- In Gal 1:10, Paul says he is a slave of Jesus because he obeys the Messiah, not seeking human approval.

- In Gal 5:13, Galatians are exhorted to "become slaves to one another," which means to serve one another.

- In 1 Corinthians 7:22–23, Paul juxtaposes "a slave of Christ" with "slaves of human masters." The former means to follow Christ, and the latter means to serve evil.

- In 1 Cor 9:19, Paul talks about his "free mission" to all, making himself a slave to all. This means he limits his freedom to serve others.

- In Phil 1:1, Paul and Timothy are called "slaves of the Messiah Jesus" because they must obey him, following his faithful humble service to God.

- In Phil 2:7–8, Paul elevates Christ Jesus as an example of an obedient life of a slave: Jesus "emptied himself, taking the form of a slave, being born in human likeness. And being found in human form, he humbled himself and became obedient to the point of death— even death on a cross."

Apostle (1:1)

Κλητὸς ἀπόστολος (*kletos apostolos*) in 1:1 is an important matter of translation. Does Paul mean he was "called to be an apostle" or that he was "an apostle called"?[12] The former indicates that his emphasis is the title of apostleship.[13] But in the case of the latter, his emphasis is not the title but the calling of God. Namely, he simply says that he is one called and sent by God

12. Jewett, *Romans*, 101.

13. In the Deutero-Pauline and Pastoral Letters, the concept and work of apostle change. Apostle has more to do with power, administration, or correct teaching. Members of the community are advised to stick together in unity without dissensions or false teachings. The apostle is a "teacher of the Gentiles in faith and truth" (1 Tim 2:7; 2 Tim 1:11; Tit 1:1). Timothy serves as a surrogate of Paul to secure a strong congregation. In this church situation, what is emphasized is correct teaching about Jesus and rigid church administration. Interestingly, there is no word of "to be called" with the apostle in the following: Eph 1:1, Col 1:1, 1 Tim 1:1, and 2 Tim 1:1.

for the gospel of God. Similarly, in Gal 1:15–16, he emphasizes his calling of God: "But when God, who had set me apart before I was born and called me through his grace, was pleased to reveal his Son to me, so that I might proclaim him among the Gentiles, I did not confer with any human being."

Paul's apostolic mission is to proclaim the gospel of God through Jesus.[14] "The gospel of God" means either the good news about God or the good news from God. In either case, the good news points to God, who is the origin and actor of the good news. God is the good news because he is righteous, steadfast and merciful. In the Hebrew Bible, God calls Abraham who was no-one to bless him, cares for all who are powerless and weak in society, and judges those who overpower the marginalized in society (Amos 5:21–24; Mic 6:8). But until Jesus came, God's good news did not work out very well because of human disobedience. But Jesus proclaimed it successfully and what he did for God's righteousness constitutes "the gospel of Christ" (c.f., 1:9).[15] In fact, in 1:3, Paul connects the gospel of God to Jesus: "the concerning his Son." Because of his faithful work for God, Jesus was declared to be Son of God (1:3–4). From Rome's perspective, Jesus failed on the cross, but in the eyes of Paul and other Christians, he did not fail. Rather he revealed who God is and what God wants: "to do justice, and to love kindness, and to walk humbly with your God" (Mic 6:8).

Because of Christ's work, Christians receive grace and apostleship (1:5). They also have to proclaim the gospel of God as Christ did, sharing it with all people. They are also apostles. While they proclaim the gospel of God through faithfulness, they must do it through Jesus's faithfulness. In other words, their gospel is to proclaim the gospel of God that was proclaimed by Jesus. In fact, Paul uses the term "my gospel" in 2:16 and 16:25.

1:5-8 THE RESULT OF THE GOSPEL

Roman Christians received grace and apostleship through Christ's love and grace. Jesus's life and his work are grace to them because he did not spare his life in revealing God's righteousness (1:4; c.f., 3:22). Because of Jesus's grace, they are also called and sent by God to do the same thing Jesus did. So they are also apostles who submit to God's righteousness. They do not do the work of God on their own, but through Christ who is guidance to

14. Brendan Byrne, *Galatians and Romans*, 59–61.

15. "The gospel of Christ" also appears in the following: 1 Cor 9:12; 2 Cor 9:13; Gal 1:7; Phil 1:27; 1 Thess 3:2.

their lives. The purpose of their apostleship is mentioned in 1:5: "to bring about the obedience of faith among all the Gentiles." "The obedience of faith" must be a genitive of origin rather than a genitive of apposition.[16] So, the emphasis is faith-obedience. That is, faith needs obedience. People have to come back to God, trusting him and following his will. For this job, Roman Christians are called. Indeed, they are called saints and God's beloved in Rome (1:6–7). They are doing well, as their faith is "proclaimed throughout the world" (1:8). Paul thanks God through Jesus because of their work.

1:9–15 PAUL'S PASSION FOR THE GOSPEL

In 1:9–15, Paul expresses his eagerness to visit Rome and to share the gospel with Roman Christians, including people in Spain. It is awkward for Paul to say this because, earlier in 1:8, he thanked God for Roman Christians' faith. They already have the gospel and proclaim it throughout Gentiles. Then, what kind of gospel does he want to share with them? Obviously, he does not claim a new gospel to them. Nevertheless, he makes sure about his gospel and his eagerness to preach it everywhere. First, in 1:9, he distinguishes between God whom he serves (namely, worships) and "the gospel of his Son" he proclaims. God is honored and worshiped by his work of evangelism, namely, by announcing "the gospel of his Son." Paul here seems to distinguish between God and Jesus his Son. "The gospel of his Son" refers to "the gospel concerning his Son" in 1:3. So, God's gospel concerning his Son must be "the gospel of his Son" in 1:9, which means the good news about Christ. Namely, Jesus brought God's good news to the world and disclosed his righteousness through faithfulness. All he did for God constitutes the good news about him. Furthermore, because of his faithfulness and righteous act, all those who follow him are given a new life in the Spirit. This is the good news about Christ.

To share this gospel of God through Christ, Paul wants to visit Rome by God's will (1:10) and to share with Roman Christians some spiritual gift to strengthen them (1:11). The spiritual gift must be his conviction about his gospel of faith, as he will elucidate it throughout Romans. As a result, their faith will be strengthened because their understanding of the gospel will be deepened. Part of his gospel conviction is shown in 1:14–15: "I am a debtor both to Greeks and to barbarians, both to the wise and to the foolish—hence my eagerness to proclaim the gospel to you also who

16. Glenn Davies, *Faith and Obedience in Romans*, 173.

are in Rome." In other words, his gospel must be preached to the end of the earth without discriminating against any determinants such as race or class. He is against the traditional Roman politics based on separation along the lines of birth, gender, class, race, nationality, or ethnicity. In the Greco-Roman world, "Greeks" means those who speak Greek or Latin and who are educated with Greco-Roman culture. "Barbarian" means all others who are "uncultured, wild, crude, fierce, and, in a basic sense, uncivilized."[17] The imperial ideology divides people into two groups: Greeks and Barbarians, or the educated and the uneducated. During the first century BCE, Spain was considered the most uncivilized barbarian country because its people were resistant to Hellenism and Rome. But Paul does not agree to this bifurcation of people and he includes in his mission the barbarians and the uneducated ("the foolish") who are treated no one. Paul's inclusion of barbarians and the foolish in his mission may seem ridiculous in the eyes of the elites who do not pay attention to any gospel other than the gospel of Caesar, which helps them to maintain their status. But Paul's gospel counters the imperial elite ideology and empowers those on the margin to live with hope in God through Christ. Paul collapses the boundary between the wise and the foolish in 1 Cor 1:26–29: "God chose what is foolish in the world to shame the wise; God chose what is weak in the world to shame the strong; God chose what is low and despised in the world, things that are not, to reduce to nothing things that are, so that no one might boast in the presence of God." All are welcome and invited to God's house through faith. For the above Gentile mission, he wants to garner some support from Roman Christians so that his future mission to Spain will be smoothed out. So, "to reap some harvest among you" in 1:13 means to win their support and understanding about his gospel mission.

1:16-17 SYNOPSIS OF THE GOSPEL

1:16–17 contains a synopsis of the gospel: "For I am not ashamed of the gospel; it is the power of God for salvation to everyone who has faith, to the Jew first and also to the Greek. For in it God's righteousness is revealed from faith to faith; as it is written, 'The one who is righteous will live by faith.'" The gospel of God or the gospel of Jesus is not the good news to the upper-class people because it is evidence of failure to them, as Jesus was crucified on the cross. But Paul says: "I am not ashamed of the gospel"

17. Jewett, *Romans*, 130–31.

because the gospel is the power of God. How is it so? On one hand, Jesus's death is tragic and looks like a failure. But for Paul, his death is the result of both his proclaiming of God's good news and his disclosing of God's righteousness. His death has to do with empowering the weak and the foolish, showing his love, grace, and faithfulness to God. On the other hand, Jesus's death for the weak and the foolish challenges the culture of honor and shame. Jesus advocated for them and because of that, he was put to death. In the Greco-Roman world, honor comes from birth, wealth, power, and success. Honor is a feeling that one receives from others because of his or her power, wisdom, and wealth. But to Jesus and Christians, honor comes from God, who cares for the foolish and the marginalized. Those who serve these people are honored by God.

As we see above, the gospel involves the power of God because God works through Jesus, the Spirit, and those who follow Jesus. This gospel is more than words about God or Jesus. Rather, the gospel brings the power of God to individuals, communities, and the world. When it is embraced by them, there will be transformation. The downtrodden will be empowered through Christ and the Spirit. Those who live in darkness must see this power of God and change their mind toward God. Salvation comes from God, not from Rome or Caesar. But it needs a response from people. Even if the sun is high above and available for all, only those who come out to receive the sunlight will live with it. Thus, what is needed for humans is faith or faithfulness. This universal theme of "salvation to everyone who has faith" is consistent in Romans.

In this power of salvation of the gospel, "the righteousness of God" (δικαιοσύν θεοῦ, *dikaiosyne theou*) has been disclosed. "The righteousness of God" is a genitive phrase, which must be a subjective genitive. In Jewish theology, as in the Old Testament, the most important claim about God is his righteousness, which may be understood through his character of love, justice, mercy, and peace.[18] It may be also understood as God's covenantal faithfulness to his people, giving of the law, sending his prophets to deliver his word, judging the evil, protecting the oppressed and the marginalized.[19]

The above aspects of God's righteousness are revealed "from faith to faith" (ἐκ πίστεως εἰς πίστιν, *ek pisteos eis pistin*). While it is not easy to pin down what the respective faith means, a good option is to read the former

18. See Katherine Grieb, *The Story of Romans*, 19–41. See also Michael Bird, *The Saving Righteousness of God*, 6–39. See also Paul Achtemeier, *Romans*, 61–65.

19. See Grieb, *The Story of Romans*, 19–41.

as Jesus's faith, and the latter as Christians' faith. As we saw before, in Paul's understanding, God's good news or his righteousness had never been fully effective because of human disobedience until Jesus came. There were many agents of God such as priests and prophets who had worked to deliver God's word. But their works have not produced satisfactory levels acceptable by God. Jesus is the one who successfully revealed God's righteousness through faithfulness. Paul thinks it is God's grace that he sent his Son Jesus to the world. By God's will, Jesus devoted his life to demonstrating God's righteousness in the world. This idea is confirmed in 3:22 in that God's righteousness has been disclosed "through Jesus Christ's faithfulness."[20] But this faithfulness of Jesus will not be effective unless there is a proper response from humans. So there is the last part in 3:22: "for all who believe or have faith" (εἰς πάντας τοὺς πιστεύοντας, *eis pantas tous pisteuontas*).

Then, in 1:17, Paul emphasizes the importance of faith and how one can be set right with God. For this emphasis, he quotes from Hab 2:4 but slightly changes it: "The one who is righteous will live by faith" (c.f., Gal 3:11; Heb 10:38). The Hebrew text of the whole verse Hab 2:4 is as follows: הִנֵּה עֻפְּלָה לֹא־יָשְׁרָה נַפְשׁוֹ בּוֹ וְצַדִּיק בֶּאֱמוּנָתוֹ יִחְיֶה, *hinneh upplah lo-yashrah napsho bo wetsadiq beemunato yichyeh*. The English translation is as follows: "Look at the proud person! His spirit is not right in him; but the one who is righteous will live by *his faith*." The difference between Rom 1:17 and the quoted Hab 2:4 (Hebrew) is that Paul omits "his" from "his faith."

In the Septuagint of Hab 2:4, we have the following: ἐὰν ὑποστείληται οὐκ εὐδοκεῖ ἡ ψυχή μου ἐν αὐτῷ ὁ δὲ δίκαιος ἐκ πίστεώς μου ζήσεται (*ean hyposteiletai ouk eudokei e psyche mou en auto ho de dikaios ek pisteos mou zesetai*). The English translation is as follows: "Look at the proud. My spirit is not right in him; but the righteous will live by *my faith*." Here the difference between 1:17 and Hab 2:4 in the Septuagint version is "my faith," which is God's faithfulness. In the Septuagint, the emphasis is people have to live by God's faith. In both the Hebrew and Septuagint texts of Hab 2:4, however, there is one thing in common: "The righteous one will live by faith," whether it is God's or a person's. Under any circumstances, the righteous person must trust God, which means to live faithfully. Therefore, the Greek text of 1:17, ὁ δὲ δίκαιος ἐκ πίστεώς ζήσεται (*ho de dikaios ek pisteos zesetai*) can be translated as "the righteous one will live by faith," not as "the righteous

20. I consider the Greek genitive διὰ πίστεως Ἰησοῦ Χριστοῦ as a subjective genitive: "through Jesus Christ's faithfulness." If Paul had meant Christians' faith in Jesus, he could have used this following form: *pistis en christo*. Therefore, it makes a better sense to read the Greek genitive as Jesus Christ's faithfulness.

one through faith will live." The latter is Luther's translation. He reads 1:17 in light of his belief about "justification by faith," juxtaposing faith with the law or works. But Paul never claims that faith is separated from deeds or works. Rather, faith means a life of faithful living by trusting and God and following Jesus. Actually, the Greek syntax does not support Luther's translation. If Paul had meant "the righteous one through faith will live," he would have had the following word order: ὁ δὲ ἐκ πίστεώς δίκαιος ζήσεται, *ho de ek pisteos dikaios zesetai*. Namely, *ek pisteos* ("by faith") is placed between *ho de* and *dikaios*. The proper translation is as follows: "the one who is righteous by faith will live." But Paul's word order is different: *ho de dikaios ek pisteos zesetai*. Here, *ek pisteos* comes before *zesetai* ("will live") and it is not placed before *dikaios* ("righteous"). Therefore, the right translation is: "The righteous one will live by faith."

In sum, in 1:17, Paul's point is that the righteous person is none other than someone who lives faithfully, based on Christ's example of love and God's grace. Justification does not happen once and for all. He/she *will* by faith, which implies that a faithful living must be ongoing. Paul's concern is not how one is declared innocent once and for all because of faith in Christ, but how one can live faithfully, participating in Christ's faith and living a new life in the Spirit. Also, his concern is to spread the good news of God to all. "To live faithfully" means that faith and works are inseparable, as James 2:26 says: "For just as the body without the spirit is dead, so faith without works is also dead." In James's Church, there were some people who interpreted faith as knowledge or conviction, saying faith alone is enough. James says Abraham and Rahab were justified by God through their works. This means faith involves works. True faith is not knowledge because even the demons believe that God exists (Jas 2:19).

SECTION II

1:18–11:36

The Gospel of Faith that Does Not Reject
the Law or Israel

1:18–3:20 THE PROBLEM OF UNFAITHFULNESS

AFTER INTRODUCING THE GOSPEL of righteousness through faith (1:1–17), Paul now discusses the real problem of humanity, as indicated in 1:18: "For the wrath of God is revealed from heaven against all ungodliness and wickedness of those who by their wickedness suppress the truth." That is, in 1:18–3:20, he deals with the problem of human disobedience or unfaithfulness to God. While the righteousness of God is revealed through faith (1:17), the wrath of God is caused by those who suppress the truth, and it is revealed now. Paul thinks of two kinds of people in the world: those who live by faith and those who live by their wickedness (unfaithfulness). For the former, God's righteousness is revealed now because of their faithfulness. For the latter, God's wrath is revealed now because of their ungodliness and wickedness. But it must be noted that the wrath of God in 1:18 should not be understood as a final verdict or judgment on those evil doers. If they accept Jesus as the Messiah and have the faithfulness of Jesus, they would experience a new life in the Spirit. Therefore, no one can judge other people even if they are crooked or evil now. Until the last day of the judgment, the gospel must be proclaimed to everyone.

For Paul, the root cause of the human problem is unfaithfulness and a darkened mind that does not respond to God's law. People knew God and the truth but suppressed the truth. The real issue for humanity is not the existence of sin but the human disobedience to God. Since sin is power, pervasive and present in the world (3:9), no one can remove it. Jesus did not remove it either, but he fought against and overcame it. Sin is still here in the world after Jesus is gone. As we will see in Rom 6–7, the only way to defeat sin is to die to it, which means not to let it exercise on to us. It is like unplugging the power code from the power source to turn off the radio. Suffice it to say now that the way to defeat sin is "to put to death the deeds of the body by the Spirit" (8:13). Sin is the power that rules the body, like the "sinful or sin-ruled body" in 6:6: "We know that our old self was crucified with him so that *the body of sin* ("the sin-ruled body") might be destroyed, and we might no longer be enslaved to sin." In other words, sin is the human condition that people cannot eradicate. Their job is to overcome the power of sin through faith or faithful living. In this sense, the human problem is not sin itself but the human crookedness and/or unwillingness to obey God. This is the topic of 1:18–3:20.

Outline of 1:18—3:20

1:18–32 The Wrath of God Because of Unfaithfulness
    1:18–23 The Wrath of God Due to Ungodliness and Wickedness
    1:24–32 The Status of Ungodly Life
2:1—3:20 All, Jews and Gentiles, Failed to Embody the Truth of God
    2:1–16 All Have Sinned, Doing Evil, Seeking Self-Glory
    2:17–29 Diatribe to Jews, Who Failed to Embody the Law of God
    3:1–8 Jewish Prerogatives and God's Faithfulness
    3:9–20 All are Under the Power of Sin

1:18–32 The Wrath of God Because of Unfaithfulness

1:18–23 The Wrath of God Due to Ungodliness and Wickedness

The particle γὰρ (*gar*) in 1:18 indicates a "marker of cause or reason" and refers to 1:16–17 in which "the righteousness of God" is revealed from faith to faith.[1] That is, if people do not live by faith, "the wrath of God" is revealed from heaven. This means that "the wrath of God" is caused by those

---

1. Walter Bauer and Frederick Danker, eds. *Greek-English Lexicon of the New Testament and Other Early Christian Literature*, 189. See also Jewett, *Romans*, 151.

who do not live by faith, as it is stated in 1:18. It is revealed (*apokaluptetai*) now, which is present passive tense. This implies God does not inflict wrath on those who do evil and suppress the truth.[2] Rather, the wrath of God is caused by humans whose thought and act are evil, which are seen in 1:19–32. Therefore, it should not be understood as God's vengeance on or permanent condemnation to those outside of the gospel. The reason is they still have time to turn to God.[3] Now is the good time that they need to return to God through faith. Now is the good time that the gospel brings the power of God for salvation to everyone through faith (1:16). Now is the good time that all are invited to the love of God through Jesus. All this implies that Paul's gospel is not the gospel of the judgment but the gospel of faith through which they are called to live a new life in the Spirit. Understood this way, therefore, *gar* ("for") does not express "its antithesis."[4] Rather, it supports "the thesis about the gospel in 1:16–17" and describes "the deplorable state of human affairs evident without the perspective of the gospel."[5]

In 1:19, Paul states no one makes excuses about his or her miserable status because God has shown plain knowledge about him. God's self-revelation is seen in his creation, as in 1:20: "Ever since the creation of the world his eternal power and divine nature, invisible though they are, have been understood and seen through the things he has made. So they are without excuse." Psalm 19:1–6 also confirms the partial knowledge of God that is manifest in his creation:

> 1 The heavens are telling the glory of God; and the firmament proclaims his handiwork. 2 Day to day pours forth speech, and night to night declares knowledge. 3 There is no speech, nor are

---

2. "Truth" must be "the truth of God," as we have this phrase in Rom 1:25. In Paul's view, God is the truth because he cares for his creation and because he is the foundation of the world and people. To him, therefore, the greatest human problem is to suppress the truth of God (1:18; 2:8, 20), which also means not to live by faith. He also says that Christ became a servant of Jews for the sake of "the truth of God" in that Gentiles are also blessed (15:8–10). In other words, God is the truth because he cares for both Jews and Gentiles.

3. Regarding the reading of divine wrath, see R. V. G. Tasker, *The Biblical Doctrine of the Wrath of God*. For more about the concept of the wrath of God, see G. H. C. Macgregor, "The Concept of the Wrath of God in the New Testament," 101–9; C. F. D. Moule, "Punishment and Retribution: An Attempt to Delimit Their Scope in New Testament Thought," 21–36.

4. Jewett, *Romans*, 151.

5. Ibid.

there words; their voice is not heard; 4 yet their voice goes out through all the earth, and their words to the end of the world. In the heavens he has set a tent for the sun, 5 which comes out like a bridegroom from his wedding canopy, and like a strong man runs its course with joy. 6 Its rising is from the end of the heavens, and its circuit to the end of them; and nothing is hid from its heat.

Paul breaks with the view of Hellenistic Judaism that humans are incapable of knowing God. This Hellenistic view is seen in Wis. 13:1: "For all people who were ignorant of God were foolish by nature; and they were unable from the good things that are seen to know the one who exists, nor did they recognize the artisan while paying heed to his works." Acts 17:22–24 also echoes this view that the Gentiles were ignorant of God:

> 22 Then Paul stood in front of the Areopagus and said, "Athenians, I see how extremely religious you are in every way. 23 For as I went through the city and looked carefully at the objects of your worship, I found among them an altar with the inscription, 'To an unknown god.' What therefore you worship as unknown, this I proclaim to you. 24 The God who made the world and everything in it, he who is Lord of heaven and earth, does not live in shrines made by human hands.

According to Acts, the Gentiles are not responsible for their past because they did not know the true God. But now they are responsible for their life because God is known to them through Christ. But this view of Acts does not match Paul's view because, in 1:18–21, he says that God revealed himself in his creation and that people knew God. He emphasizes that humans cannot make excuses about their unfaithfulness because God manifested himself to them, as he says in 1:21: "for though they knew God, they did not honor him as God or give thanks to him, but they became futile in their thinking, and their senseless minds were darkened." People knew God but they did not honor him as God because they were futile in their thinking and "they exchanged the glory of the immortal God for images resembling a mortal human being or birds or four-footed animals or reptiles" (1:23). Because humans are self-focused with burning passions about success and fame, there is no God in their mind and behavior. They do not distinguish between "the glory of the immortal God" and images resembling things in his creation. Ironically, "claiming to be wise, they became fools" (1:22).[6]

---

6. This kind of irony about human wisdom or strength is also stated in 1 Cor 1:25: "For God's foolishness is wiser than human wisdom, and God's weakness is stronger than

1:24–32 The Status of Ungodly Life

In 1:24–32, Paul lists more examples of ungodly life and human depravity. He mentions three times the formula "God gave them up" (1:24, 26, 28). First, in 1:24, he states that "God gave them up in the lusts of their hearts to impurity, to the degrading of their bodies among themselves." God's giving them up to impurity and to the degrading of their bodies among themselves happened in the past (παρέδωκεν, *paredoken*, an aorist verb of "to give up") and continues to happen now.[7] They live according to their lusts and do whatever they want with their bodies.

Second, in 1:26, Paul also says: "For this reason God gave them up to degrading passions." Here the issue is degrading passions, which are related to the lusts in their hearts. Then, Paul lists examples of degrading passions in the case of women's homosexual relations (1:26) and men's homosexual relations (1:27). Obviously, he condemns these homosexual relations. But the question is: Does he rule out all forms of homosexual relations? Or, does he condemn particular forms of homosexual relations? Some think Paul prohibits all forms of homosexual relations, be they abusive or loving in mutual relations. Church fathers such as Chrysostom and Clement of Alexandria also believe that Paul prohibits all kinds of homosexual relations. This view is based on the following: 1) "against nature" (παρὰ φύσιν, *para physin*) must be understood in the context of God's creation in which heterosexual marriage is intended by God from beginning;[8] 2) Jewish tradition in Paul's time rejected homosexual relations no matter what;[9] 3) Greco-Roman writers also applied "against nature" to same-sex eroticism.[10] But other scholars suggest that Paul only talks about specific

---

human strength."

7. Jewett, *Romans*, 157, n. 19.

8. In this view, God created humans and made different genders for a purpose. Therefore, the violation of gender roles in sexual relations is "against nature" (παρὰ φύσιν, *para physin*).

9. Purity is an important concern for Jews, and homosexual relations are considered impure.

10. Plato, *Laws*, 636B–D: "The sexual pleasure experienced by the female and male natures when they join together for the purpose of procreation seems to have been handed down in accordance with nature, whereas the pleasure enjoyed by males with males and females with females seems to be beyond nature (*para physin*), and the boldness of those who first engaged in this practice seems to have arisen out of an inability to control pleasure." Also, later Jewish and Stoic writers such as Philo, Josephus, Seneca the Younger, and Plutarch applied the concept of *para physin* to homoerotic behavior. See

acts of homosexual relations. In other words, the issue is heterosexuals who have homosexual sex.[11] Others think the real issue is pederasty or abusive relationships, and Paul does not prohibit all types of homosexual relations, which are widespread in Greco-Roman society.[12]

Still others point out the problem of the excessive desire (lust), as Fredrickson observes: "Romans 1:24–27 is not an attack on homosexuality as a violation of divine law but a description of the human condition informed by the philosophic rejection of passionate love."[13] Brownson also says similarly: "It is not desire itself that Paul opposes, but excessive desire, which directs itself toward what is not rightly ours, overcoming self-control and obedience to God."[14] In this view, "unnatural sex" is not the same as homoeroticism, but it has to do with the excessive desire, whether in heterosexual or same-sex relations. In my view, Paul condemns abusive, lustful, idolatrous homosexual activities caused by degrading passions. Otherwise, we do not know whether he, just like other Jewish teachers, condemned all forms of homosexual relations. While his condemnation of all kinds of homoeroticism is not implausible given his Jewish background, it may be also possible for him not to condemn all homosexual activities because, as a Hellenistic Jew, he knows the diversity of sexual relations in the Greco-Roman world. Then, given this complexity about 1:26–27, what can we say about modern-day sexual ethics and homosexuality? In 1:18–32, it does not seem that Paul talks about homosexuality as a sole topic that is important on its own. Rather, his main topics are the wrath of God, human disobedience to God, and its result appearing in manifestations of human crookedness and senseless mind. In this literary context of 1:18–32, Paul has an issue with a specific type of homosexuality caused by idolatry and degrading passions. In other words, he does not seem to talk about loving relationships in same-sex relationships. Therefore, it is hard to apply 1:26–27 to modern-day homosexuality discussion. In some sense, from his perspective, the real issue is not whether one has heterosexual or

Plutarch, *Moralia* 990 E–F.

11. John Boswell, *Christianity, Social Tolerance, and Homosexuality*. See also Dale Martin, *Sex and the Single Savior*.

12. Robin Scroggs, *New Testament and Homosexuality*, 85–98.

13. David Fredrickson, "Natural and Unnatural Use in Romans 1:24–27: Paul and the Philosophic Critique of Eros," 208.

14. James Brownson, *Bible, Gender, Sexuality*, 164.

homosexual tendency but how one truly loves God and neighbor. That is, the issue is how to recover faithfulness to God.

Lastly, in 1:28, Paul uses the same formula "God gave them up." In this time, his emphasis is on "a debased mind" and all kinds of evil thinking and deeds, as listed in 1:29–31: "29 They were filled with every kind of wickedness, evil, covetousness, malice. Full of envy, murder, strife, deceit, craftiness, they are gossips, 30 slanderers, God-haters, insolent, haughty, boastful, inventors of evil, rebellious toward parents, 31 foolish, faithless, heartless, ruthless." In 1:32, Paul once again emphasizes the human knowledge of God's decree, as he did in 1:18–21. But the problem is they were unfaithful to God and practiced evil in its all forms. Those who practice evil things "deserve to die—yet they not only do them but even applaud others who practice them" (1:32).

2:1—3:20 All, Jew and Gentile, Failed to Embody the Truth of God

2:1-16 All Have Sinned, Doing Evil, Seeking Self-Glory

In 2:1—3:20, interlocutors appear as his imaginative dialogue partners. "You" refers to Jews and Gentiles. Here Paul explains why all people, Jews and Gentiles, failed to embody the truth of God. In 2:1-16, he states that all have sinned, doing evil, seeking self-glory. The interlocutors in 2:1-8 are not specified. But we know what kind of people they are. They judge others while doing the same things that they condemn. They say: "We know that God's judgment on those who do such things is in accordance with truth" (2:2). They judge others in the name of God and condemning them. By their judgment, they block them from receiving God's kindness through which they may lead to repentance (*metanoia*, which means to change a mind) (2:4-5).

According to Paul's gospel, God is patient and kind to all (c.f., 1:16–17; 3:21–26). Therefore, in 2:4, he asks: "Or do you despise the riches of his kindness and forbearance and patience?" His point is God's judgment is not final yet; there is still time for repentance and transformation. The day of wrath as a final judgment will come when "God's righteous judgment will be revealed" (2:5). "God's righteous judgment" is based on each one's deeds, not by word. In fact, those who judge others while doing the same things themselves are much more miserable because by their judgment they missed the opportunity to repent. Eventually, on the last day, there will be a division between eternal life and fury. 2:8–10 states well about this: "while for those who are self-seeking and who obey not the truth but wickedness, there will be wrath and fury. There will be anguish and distress for everyone who does evil, the Jew first and also the Greek, but glory and honor and peace for everyone who does good, the Jew first and also the Greek."

God's righteous judgment applies to both Jews and Gentiles because both groups failed to do good works. "All who have sinned apart from the law" are Gentiles, and "all who have sinned under the law" are Jews. Both groups have sinned, which means they did not live by faith. For Jews, they heard the law but did not do righteous things in God's sight, as 2:13 states: "For it is not the hearers of the law who are righteous in God's sight, but the doers of the law who will be justified." The ultimate judgment is done by God, and one's action must be seen righteous in God's sight. Gentiles do not have the law, but they cannot be excused from God's judgment because their nature tells them between what is right and what is wrong. Paul says: "what the law requires is written on their hearts, to which their own conscience also bears witness; and their conflicting thoughts will accuse or perhaps excuse them" (2:15). Thus, on the day of wrath, they cannot avoid God's righteous judgment because their secret thoughts are revealed (2:16).

2:17–29 Diatribe to Jews Who Failed to Embody the Law of God

In 2:17–29, Paul emphasizes how Jews failed to embody the law [of God], stating that their ethnic identity based on the law and their special relation to God (as descendants of Abraham) are of no value to them if they do not understand and practice the law in an authentic sense that God approves. In other words, if they do not care for the orphans, widows, and foreigners, their knowledge of God is nothing. Likewise, claiming to know the truth of God is also nothing. God is the truth because he saves the world through mercy and justice. Accordingly, they must participate in God's salvific work in the world, so that the Gentiles may see the good works of them. The law must be served for that purpose. God's name is blasphemed among the Gentiles if they do not do what God requires them to do (c.f., Mic 6:8). In that case, their boasting in the law is invalid and leads to dishonoring God (2:23). Likewise, circumcision must be understood well (2:25–29). The true value of circumcision is inwardly and spiritual. This idea seems to derive from Jer 4:4: "Circumcise yourselves to the LORD, remove the foreskin of your hearts, O people of Judah and inhabitants of Jerusalem, or else my wrath will go forth like fire, and burn with no one to quench it, because of the evil of your doings." All this implies that the circumcised must be transformed, as he says in 2:29: "Rather, a person is a Jew who is one inwardly, and real circumcision is a matter of the heart." This idea of transformation appears again in 12:1–2: "I appeal to you therefore, brothers and sisters, by the mercies of God, to present your bodies as a living sacrifice, holy and acceptable to God, which is your spiritual worship. Do not be conformed to this world, but be transformed by the renewing of your minds, so that you may discern what is the will of God—what is good and acceptable and perfect."

3:1–8 Jewish Prerogatives and God's Faithfulness

But Paul warns the Gentiles that they should not despise Jews because they are God's covenanted people (3:1–2). Circumcision has much value because it is a special sign of children of God. Moreover, if circumcision is rightly understood, it has transformative value that they have to commit to spiritual life to God, as Jeremiah says: "Circumcise yourselves to the LORD, remove the foreskin of your hearts" (Jer 4:4). But as we know, not all Jews were faithful enough to God. So Paul asks: "What if some were unfaithful? Will their faithlessness nullify the faithfulness of God?" (3:3). The answer is: "By no means!" (3:4). This means God is faithful to his people for good. He will find a way for them to be saved. This issue is dealt with later in Rom 9–11.

Then, in 3:5–8, Paul deals with several related issues regarding God's faithfulness to his faithless people. Some say God is unjust because "our injustice serves to confirm the justice of God." In other words, they say that God is not justice because he allows for human injustices. Then Paul raises another question: "That God is unjust to inflict wrath on us? (I speak in a human way)" (3:5). In other words, how can a good God inflict wrath on us? The answer is "By no means! For then how could God judge the world?" (3:6). In other words, he affirms the wrath of God because there must be an ultimate judgment of people. In 3:7–8, Paul goes back to the issue of God's justice in 3:5 where the question is: How can people say God is justice if sinners or injustice is allowed to him? In 3:7–8, some think that they may do more evil or sin more because God's grace or truthfulness will abound. But Paul's answer is simple: "Their condemnation is deserved!" (3:8). This implies that even though God is gracious and patient, the abuse of his grace is not tolerant.

3:9–20 All Are Under the Power of Sin

In this section, Paul summarizes the issue of the human problem, which is unfaithfulness. But this unfaithfulness is universal because it is caused by sin. So he asks his interlocutors, Jews, who have God's prerogatives such as the law or covenant: "What then? Are we any better off?" His answer is: "No, not at all; for we have already charged that all, both Jews and Greeks, are under the power of sin" (3:9). "The power of sin" is the ultimate root cause of the human problem. It fills the world and humans, as he cites from various scriptures in 3:10–18. Here humanity is pictured very negatively; all are sinful and evil. On the one hand, it is people's problem because they are evil. But on the other hand, it is sin's power under which they are controlled. This issue of the human predicament is dealt with throughout Rom 3–8, especially in 6:1–23. From the outset, it must be said that he does not suggest that sin can be completely removed from us or from the world or that sin's power was defeated by Jesus once and for all. Rather, it still remains in the world. Often, 3:10–18 is read as the doctrine of universal sin or total human depravity that the solution comes through Jesus's redemptive, vicarious death for sin atonement. In other words, the doctrine assumes that sin can be removed from an individual or from the world. But that is not true because sin as power remains even after Jesus was resurrected. Nevertheless, this doctrine reads 3:21–26 as a solution to sin's problem because Jesus became "a sacrifice of atonement." The doctrine also says those who have faith in Jesus will be justified by God and freed from sin. But this traditional view will be challenged, as we will see later. Suffice it to say, in 3:10–18, Paul emphasizes the hopeless situation of humanity due to the power of sin.

Then in 3:19, he says: "Now we know that whatever the law says, it speaks to those who are under the law, so that every mouth may be silenced, and the whole world may be held accountable to God." In other words, sin as power is not the only problem because there is the law by which Jews and others know what is right and what is wrong. Here the law is a general law, close to the revelation of God in nature and human conscience. On the one hand, the law is needed to protect life and maintain order in the community. Romans and Jews must keep the law and behave accordingly.

But there will be a consequence of their action: "so that every mouth may be silenced, and the whole world may be held accountable to God." This implies that every law, Jewish or not, must be kept responsibly to establish a community of justice that God approves.

Then in 3:20a, Paul says: "For no human being will be justified in his sight by *works of the law (ἐξ ἔργων νόμου, eks ergon nomou)*." However, this verse should not be read from the perspective of a dichotomy between the law and faith. Judaism in first-century Palestine was not a legalistic religion. In other words, Jews do not keep the law to earn favor from God or to gain righteousness. They believe they already became children of God. They keep the law to stay in the covenantal community and thank God for their salvation.[15]

The issue is "works of the law" such as purity rules and other rituals that are important to Jewish identity.[16] While these works are important to Jews, they have to extend the love of God to others without conditions. Otherwise, they will not be justified in God's sight. Here "works of the law" may also refer to the legal system in the Roman Empire where Romans are classified according to their achievement or power.[17] The strong prosper at the sacrifice of the weak. It is not right with God because the former does not do justice.

In 3:20b, Paul explains why the narrow, selfish view of the law causes a big problem: "for through the law comes *the knowledge of sin*." Often, "the knowledge of sin" is often understood from the perspective a dichotomy between the law and faith. In this view, the law brings the knowledge of sin, convicting people of their sins because no one keeps the law perfectly. Luther thought this way, saying he discovered a way out of this predicament due to the impossibility of the law. The solution is by faith, not by keeping the law. But this view is not held by Paul who never claims that the law is sinful or imperfect. Rather, the law is holy and God's commandments are perfect (7:12). Jesus did not repeal the law but he fulfilled it (10:4). Paul well summarizes the commandments: "Love your neighbor as yourself. Love does no wrong to a neighbor; therefore, love is the fulfilling of the law. 'Owe no one anything, except to love one another; for the one who loves another has fulfilled the law.'" (13:9–10).

15. See E.P. Sanders, *Paul and Palestinian Judaism*, 420.

16. James Dunn, *The New Perspective on Paul*, 111.

17. Jewett, *Romans*, 266.

Then, what is "the knowledge of sin"? This may be best understood as "the sinful knowledge" or "the sin-ruled knowledge" in a specific context of the law. In the Jewish context, sinful knowledge occurs when they absolutize part of the law and forget the universal love of God for all people. In the Roman context, Jewett explains about this: "The knowledge that traditional systems of achieving honor and avoiding shame are sinful and must be abandoned."[18] Overall, as Jewett also observes, the issue is "not a matter of failure to perform the law, but as Rom 7 will explain in detail, a matter of sinful competition that turns conformity to law into a means of status acquisition."[19]

The sinful competition and the sinful knowledge can be dealt with properly, as we will see from 6:10: "The death he died, he died to sin, once for all; but the life he lives, he lives to God." This also means people have to "put to death the deeds of the body by the Spirit" (8:13). 6:6 is also helpful: "We know that our old self was crucified with him so that the body of sin might be destroyed, and we might no longer be enslaved to sin."

3:21–4:25 RIGHTEOUSNESS THROUGH CHRIST'S FAITHFULNESS

In 3:21–4:25, Paul defends the gospel of faith, which is about God's righteousness that comes through Jesus Christ's faithfulness. The gist of the gospel is well expressed in 3:21–22: "But now, apart from law, God's righteousness has been disclosed, and is attested by the law and the prophets, God's righteousness Jesus Christ's faithfulness for all who believe. For there is no distinction." "Apart from law" (χωρὶς νόμου, *choris nomou*) does not mean that Jewish law is useless or nothing. Rather, God's righteousness is attested by the law and the prophets. "But now, apart from law" implies that God's righteousness has been disclosed in a non-traditional way or unexpectedly in human history. Because of his Son's faithfulness, God put forward him as "a new place of reconciliation."[20] That is, people can be reconciled with God when they come to recognize Jesus's faithfulness and participate in it (3:26). Thus 3:24 says: "They are now justified by his grace as a gift, through the redemption that is in Christ Jesus." Because of

18. Jewett, *Romans*, 266.

19. Ibid., 267.

20. "A new place of reconciliation" implies that Jesus is not the only place of reconciliation with God because people may come to God through the Holy Spirit.

Jesus's faithful life and his "moral sacrifice,"[21] God dealt with the sins previously committed and opened a new path of reconciliation through faith.[22] However, Paul affirms that the law cannot be overthrown by faith, because when the former is discerned by the latter, it guides people into the right path. Thus the law must be upheld and it is holy (3:31; 7:12). The problem of Jews is not the law per se but their unbelief that Jesus is the Messiah as well as their zeal for God. The law cannot take the place of God. It must be guided by faith in God. God's promise or grace comes first. Then the grace of God is accepted by faith. God is the God of both the circumcised and the uncircumcised. All of them can be justified through the same faith. Otherwise, "works of the law" will not make a person stand holy and perfect before God. What really matters is "the law of faith," which means that faith informs the law. Faith means trusting God and depending solely on his grace as a gift.

Then, in 4:1–25, Paul proves his case of the gospel of faith by talking about Abraham's faith. Abraham trusted God and walked along the road of faith through the ups and downs in his life. He did not give up on his journey until dying. His faith was reckoned to him as righteousness. His faith depends on the grace of God and his promise. He was circumcised after he followed God. The law was given later through Moses. For Paul, this order is important: from God's grace or promise to faith and to the law. What is required of God's people is to live by faith (c.f., 1:17; Hab 2:4). This faith must guide the adherents of the law. Circumcision is "a seal of

21. The concept of "moral sacrifice" in this book has to do with Jesus's faithfulness to God. Because of his work of God, he was put to death. His death therefore does not have to do with sin-offering.

22. When it comes to Jesus's death and its implications, it is important to distinguish between "moral sacrifice" and "sacrificial, sin-offering." The latter is the view of the traditional atonement theories. But the former emphasizes Jesus's work for God's righteousness. Brondos sees Jesus's death as a result of his work and faithfulness to God. See David Brondos, *Paul on the Cross: Reconstructing the Apostle's Story of Redemption* (Minneapolis: Fortress, 2006), 63–190. Daniel Patte, in his forthcoming volume 2 on Romans (T&T Clark), lists three kinds of atonement interpretation in 3:22–26: (1) ἱλαστήριον as a propitiation/expiation, based on a forensic theological interpretation, which emphasizes the need for appeasing God's anger; (2) as a covenantal sacrifice that removes sins and purifies people (here the issue is the ungodliness and wickedness as in 1:18); (3) as a redemption that emphasizes the need of liberation/freedom from bondage to sin or from evil or from idolatry. About the traditional atonement theories, see Gustaf Aulén, *Christus Victor: A Historical Study of the Three Main Types of the Idea of the Atonement,* trans. A. G. Hebert (London: SPCK, 1945). See also Adam J. Johnson, ed. *T&T Clark Companion to Atonement* (New York: T&T Clark, 2017).

the righteousness that he [Abraham] had by faith while he was still uncircumcised" (4:11). Now, like Abraham, those who believe in God who raised Jesus from the dead will be saved (c.f., 10:9). For Paul, strictly speaking, the object of faith and worship is God, as he states in 4:24: "It will be reckoned to us who believe in him who raised Jesus our Lord from the dead" (c.f., 1:9).

Outline of 3:21—4:25

3:21–26   God's righteousness through Christ's faithfulness
        for all who have faith

    3:21–23   God's righteousness through Christ's faithfulness for all

    3:24–26   God's righteousness proven through Christ's faithfulness and
        his moral sacrifice

3:27–31   Justification by the law of faith, not by the works
        of the law

    3:27–28   By the law of faith, not by works of the law

    3:29–30   Since God is one, both Jews and Gentiles are justified
        through the same faith

    3:31   But the law cannot be overthrown by faith

4:1–25   Abraham as the father of faith for all, Jews and Gentiles

    4:1–5   Abraham's faith, not his works, considered as righteousness

    4:6–8   David's testimony about God's grace as a gift

    4:9–12   Righteousness through Abraham's faith,
        before his circumcision

    4:13–15   The promise through the righteousness of faith, not through
        the adherents of the law

    4:16–17   The promise/grace of God through faith for all, the adherents
        of the law and Gentiles

    4:18–22   The proof of Abraham's faith

    4:23–25   Abraham's case applying to followers of Jesus who believe in
        God

3:21–26 God's righteousness through Christ's faithfulness for all who have faith

3:21–23 God's righteousness through Christ's faithfulness for all

"But now" (Νυνὶ δὲ, *nuni de*) in 3:21 hints a logical antithesis against 1:18–20, a section that humanity failed thoroughly because of sin's power and sinful passions. More than that, it also emphasizes the realized time of God's righteousness, which was disclosed through Jesus Christ's faithfulness. The notion of "now" echoes Jesus's initial preaching in Mark 1:14–15 that he began to proclaim the good news of God after John the Baptist was arrested. His message is that God's time has been fulfilled. Now is the time that people must turn to God. It is Jesus's consciousness that the time of salvation is now when they must change their minds toward God. Likewise, it is Paul's understanding that God's righteousness has been disclosed through Jesus who boldly proclaimed the good news of God to disclose his righteousness. However, the caution is, "but now" does not replace Judaism and introduce a new system of salvation apart from the law. In fact, God's good news has been promised through his prophets in the holy Scriptures (1:2) and his righteousness is attested by the law and the prophets (3:21).

In this time of "now," we also see God's initiative in terms of his saving activity or sovereignty over the world.[23] In biblical history, God is acting toward justice, ruling and judging the world with righteousness, as in the LXX Ps 97:7–9: "Let the sea be moved, and all that fills it; the world and those who dwell in it! Let the rivers clap their hands; let the hills sing for joy together for he comes to rule the earth. He will judge the world with righteousness, and the peoples with uprightness."[24] In this regard, "the righteousness of God" (*dikaiosyne theou*) must be a subjective genitive.[25]

In sum, "but now" connotes two important things. First, God's righteousness has been distinctly manifested now through Jesus who revealed God's righteousness. Because of his faithful sacrifice for God and the world, Jesus was declared to be Son of God (1:4). Second, it is now that God's

---

23. See Jewett, *Romans*, 272–75; Ernst Käsemann, *New Testament Questions of Today*, 180; Peter Stuhlmacher, *Reconciliation, Law, & Righteousness*, 81.

24. Jewett, *Romans*, 272–3. See also John J. Scullion, "Righteousness (OT)," 735.

25. Jewett observes well about this: "It is not so much the individual soul that is at stake in the revelation of divine righteousness that occurred in Christ and the subsequent preaching of the gospel, but rather the restoration of the entire cosmic order, including each group and species distorted by sin." See Jewett, *Romans*, 273.

righteousness has been disclosed through faith, not based on the law or works of the law. Paul argues that this faith is not a new concept but a scriptural concept that has been operative since Abraham. We will explore more about this in 3:27–31 and 4:1–25.

"Apart from law" (χωρὶς νόμου, *choris nomou*, without the definite article before the law") must be a better translation as in the NRSV than "apart from the law." In other words, Jewish law is not primarily referred to here because it is holy and testifies about God's righteousness (3:22). Therefore, we think χωρὶς νόμου (*choris nomou*) modifies the verb "to manifest." That is, God's righteousness has been disclosed extraordinarily, or beyond the law or any laws. It was revealed through his Son, Jesus Christ's faithfulness. God's righteousness has been manifested "in a revolutionary manner through Christ."[26] In other words, God's righteousness is disclosed universally without the law or beyond the laws, which means "outside the national and religious parameters set by the law, without reference to the normal Jewish hallmarks."[27]

After clarifying the timing ("but now") and manner ("apart from law") of God's righteousness, Paul drives home his threefold gospel, as in 3:22–23: "God's righteousness through the faith of Jesus Christ for all who believe. For there is no distinction, since all have sinned and fall short of the glory of God."[28] In the threefold gospel, three participating subjects stand out: God's righteousness, Jesus Christ's faithfulness and all those who have faith. God's righteousness means God's initiative in terms of his saving activity. Namely, God is righteous, merciful, steadfast and loving. Jesus Christ's faithfulness is the translation of πίστεως Ἰησοῦ Χριστοῦ, *pisteos Iesou Christou*, in 3:22, which is considered a subjective genitive meaning.[29] If Paul had meant "faith in Jesus Christ" (an objective genitive meaning), there would be no need of the last part: "for those who have faith" because it is redundant. As Luke Timothy Johnson observes, the *pistis* genitive in 3:22 must be a subjective genitive because another *pistis* genitive in 3:26 (πίστεως Ἰησοῦ, *pisteos Iesou*) has the personal name Jesus which emphasizes Jesus's humanity.[30] This kind of subjective translation is also found in reference to

---

26. Jewett, *Romans*, 274.

27. James Dunn, *Romans*, Vol. 1, 165.

28. For more about a threefold theology of Paul, see Kim, *A Theological Introduction to Paul's Letters*.

29. Johnson, *Reading Romans*, 59–62.

30. Johnson, *Reading Romans*, 60. The examples that emphasize Jesus's humanity are

Abraham's faith, as the NRSV translates it well: "those who share the faith of Abraham."[31] Here, Abraham is the subject of faith. Furthermore, if Paul had meant "faith in Christ," he could have used the prepositional phrase *pistis en christo* (which means "faith in Christ"). Paul's point is Jesus was faithful to God, disclosing his righteousness at the risk of his life.

The last participating subject in the threefold gospel is Christians ("those who have faith"). Even if God's righteousness came through Christ's faithfulness, it cannot become effective for them unless they participate in his faithfulness. That is, they must accept the good news of God and live by faith—in imitation of Christ. Then, they may live in the Spirit. This concept of faith goes beyond "an individual's intellectual, emotional, or existential stance."[32] In an intellectual stance, Jesus is understood as the object of faith.[33] One must believe in him; that is all necessary for justification and salvation. In an emotional level, for example, faith is "the attitude of pure receptivity in which the soul appropriates what God has done."[34] In an existential stance, Rudolf Bultmann's position is typical. For him, faith is "a radical decision of the will in which man delivers himself up."[35] But all of the above aspects of faith do not take on the ethical dimension of faith. That is, for Paul, faith means to trust God and participate in God's good news or his righteousness. Accordingly, faith means to follow Jesus.

In this threefold gospel, the common ground is faith. Indeed, God is the most faithful character in the Bible. God's faithful commitment to his covenant with Israelites does not change in Jewish scriptures. God's faithfulness to the salvation of all peoples is also emphasized by Paul. For example, he says in 1 Cor 1:9: "God is faithful; by him you were called into the fellowship of his Son, Jesus Christ our Lord." The Corinthians were called into the sharing of Jesus Christ's faithfulness and his death. But this sharing of Jesus Christ is possible because of God's faithfulness. In other words, God sent his Son Jesus to save humanity and Jesus was faithful to him. Here we see Jesus Christ's faithfulness to God. Likewise, people must show their faithfulness to God through Jesus, which means they should imitate Christ.

---

as follows: Rom 8:11; 1 Thess 1:10; 2 Cor 4:10–14.

31. Johnson, *Reading Romans*, 60.

32. Jewett, *Romans*, 277. Jewett includes good examples of each of this stance.

33. Heinrich Meyer, *Critical and Exegetical Handbook to the Epistle to the Romans*, 1:164; John Murray, *The Epistle to the Romans*, 111.

34. C. H. Dodd, *The Epistle of Paul to the Romans*, 56.

35. Rudolf Bultmann, "pisteuo ktl," 219–20.

3:24–26 God's Righteousness Proven through Christ's Faithfulness and His Moral Sacrifice

The following is my translation of 3:24–26:

> 24 They are now justified by his grace as a gift, through the redemption that is in Christ Jesus, 25 whom God put forward as a new place of reconciliation by his blood and through his faithfulness. He did this to show his righteousness, because in his divine forbearance he had passed over the sins previously committed; 26 it was to prove at the present time that he himself is righteous and that he justifies the one who has the faithfulness of Jesus.

In 3:24, Christians are set right with God by his grace as a gift. One's right relationship with God starts with God's grace, not with an individual's faith. This is very clear in Abraham's case too. God called him out of nowhere, and Abraham trusted him. Likewise, Paul acknowledges God's initiative of grace, which must be the basis of one's right relationship with God. But God's grace is not the final thing for justification because there must be a proper response called faith. Since Abraham was called, his descendants have never been faithful to God. That is Paul's understanding. This is where God's Son, Jesus, is introduced. Namely, in 3:24, justification is possible "through the redemption that is in Christ Jesus." It needs Jesus's work that is called the redemption (ἀπολύτρωσις, *apolytrosis*), which connotes various things: freedom from captivity, release from the devil with a ransom, freedom from slavery, forgiveness of sins, or being freed from sin. Among these, "being freed from sin or from evil" may be the best option to consider, because sinning is pointed out as the main problem of people in 3:23: "all have sinned and fall short of the glory of God." But Jesus defeated the power of sin by dying to sin (6:10) and did not become a slave of sin. Therefore, those who follow him also have to do the same thing, dying to sin, not following their sinful passions. Likewise, they have to put to death the deeds of the body by the Spirit (8:13). In this sense, their redemption (in the sense of liberation from sin or evil) does not come by Jesus's death alone but through their participation in his faithfulness.

In 3:25, Jesus's work of redemption is connected with ἱλαστήριον (*hilasterion*), which has been the topic of scholarly debate for a long time. By and large, three types of interpretation are widespread in history. The traditional one is based on the Jewish festival of Yom Kippur where God is present on the cover of the ark of the covenant (Exod 25:17–22), which is called *ha kapporet.* With this cultic Jewish setting, Paul thinks that God's mercy is found on Jesus, who is the place of atonement. Jesus' sacrifice and his blood are necessary to the atonement. So usually, *hilasterion* is translated as "a sacrifice of atonement" (for example, in the NRSV and the NIV).[36] The assumption here is that Jesus is a sin offering. Understood this way, there is no difference between 3:25 and Hebrews 10:12: "But when Christ had offered for all time a single sacrifice for sins, "he sat down at the right hand of God." In this line of thought, Jesus' death is a sin-offering that supports the atonement theory of penal substitution. Or, it may be a price of ransom (ransom theory) that a person is released from the hands of the devil. Or, it may be a price to satisfy God's moral standard that requires a perfect sacrifice of a sinless person. In all of this, Jesus' death is needed to deal with sins in one way or another. The above view of Jesus' death is widespread among scholars, as James Dunn also states: "At all events it is the God who provided the sacrificial cult for Israel who also put forward Christ as the decisive sin offering for all who believe."[37] The other similar interpretation of *hilasterion* is to emphasize "propitiation" by Jesus' sacrifice that relieves God from his wrath.[38] In a pagan cultic setting, *hilasterion* usually means propitiation, which has to do with allaying the angry god by offering him or her a gift or sacrifice. Likewise, God is satisfied with this kind of sacrifice by Jesus. But the burden of this interpretation is about God's character. The question is: How a good God allow for such a horrendous death of his Son?

Therefore, we need an alternative interpretation of *hilasterion*, not based on the image of Jesus' sacrifice itself, but based on Jesus' faithfulness and his moral sacrifice for God's righteousness. We can begin by

36. Ἱλαστήριον in Rom 3:25 is usually translated as "a sacrifice of atonement" (for example, in the NRSV and NIV) whose image relates to the tradition of Yom Kippur in the Old Testament. As blood is sprinkled on "the cover of the ark of the covenant," Jesus's blood is shed on the cross. In this view, Jesus is a sacrificial victim, and his death is a sin-offering. Other views of ἱλαστήριον include the following: (1) ἱλαστήριον as propitiation to God with its usage extracted from Hellenistic culture or from some Jewish context; (2) as an expiation, the price for repairing the broken relationship between God and humanity; (3) as a place of divine presence like "the mercy seat" (תְרְפַכַה) on Yom Kippur. By and large, all of these views associate ἱλαστήριον with the cultic image of sacrifice, whether its usage is drawn from Hellenistic culture or from Yom Kippur.

37. Dunn, *Romans*, 181.

38. Propitiation is based on a forensic interpretation of salvation. That is, the issue is "God's wrath" against sinners, as seen in 1:18 (ὀργὴ θεοῦ). The solution is to placate God's wrath and the right means is Jesus's death. As a result, those who believe in Jesus will not be punished. For more about the forensic interpretation, see Daniel Patte, *Romans*, forthcoming. This idea of propitiation is found 4 Maccabees 17:21–22.

reinterpreting the meaning of atonement on Yom Kippur. Atonement means "at-one-ment," a concept of reconciliation between God and humanity.[39] As a history of interpretation shows, atonement has been understood variously: 1) Sins are to dealt with first, and then sinners can be restored to God (Jesus's sin-offering);[40] 2) the wrath of God must be dealt with first (Jesus's death as a propitiation); 3) there must be an expiation to mend the broken relationship (Jesus's death as expiation).[41] But an alternative view is to see *hilasterion* as a place of reconciliation because of Jesus's faithfulness and his moral sacrifice. To help understand this, we can reinterpret the meaning of *ha kapporet* on the Day of Atonement. Israelites gather on Yom Kippur and come to the high priest to be atoned for their sins when animals are sacrificed and blood is sprinkled on the cover. One may think that their sins are forgiven and they are restored to God because guilt and sins are transferred to animals. But in true religiosity what is more important is not animal sacrifice or the sprinkled blood but their repentance or changing of their mind toward God. The blood or sacrifice is a ritual or symbol that must come with the change of their mind. God's mercy seat is available not because of the blood or sacrifice but because of people's coming to God with repentance. Then their sins are forgiven and they are reconciled with God.

Given the above interpretation of the story on Yom Kippur, Paul does not think a mere sacrifice of Jesus would be enough for reconciliation between God and humanity. Rather, he sees Jesus's faithfulness on the cross and his moral sacrifice for God's righteousness. Jesus's faithfulness means he devoted his life to disclosing God's righteousness in the world (3:22). His death is a tragic one and yet it is a moral sacrifice out of his faithfulness that God must be the ruler of the earth. God is righteous, merciful, steadfast and caring. Jesus proclaimed the good news of God until he died. God was impressed by his Son's faithfulness.[42] Therefore, God put forward

---

39. See Frank J. Matera, "Reconciliation," 856.

40. Jesus's death as sin-offering or for the forgiveness of sins may be found in Hebrews 10:10 and 1 Pet 3:18. The use of ἱλαστήριον in Heb 9:5 is very different from Rom 3:25. In Hebrews, the old covenant and the old purification are imperfect and obsolete (Heb 9: 3–15; 10:1), and Jesus replaces the old system of the law and sacrifices (Heb 10:11–14).

41. See C. H. Dodd, *The Bible and the Greeks*. See also James Dunn, *Romans 1–8*, 170, 176–183; Käsemann, *Commentary on Romans*, 91–101.

42. In Paul's view, Jesus's death reveals the character of God. In other words, the cross represents the love of God because it shows Jesus's lifelong sacrificial work of God. See Charles Cousar, *A Theology of the Cross*, 25–51.

him as "a new place of reconciliation." Jesus proved that God is righteous. Jesus becomes a mercy seat and reconciliation for whoever comes to him and repent.

From the above understanding of *hilasterion*, "by his blood" in 3:25 is a representing word about Jesus's moral sacrifice. In other words, it means the cost of his lifelong work for God, including his crucifixion. So, "by his blood" does not necessarily refer to the sacrificial blood on the cross.[43] Also, "through faith" (διὰ πίστεως, *dia pisteos*) in 3:25 must be the faithfulness of Jesus.[44] It is not the believer's faith in Jesus's sacrifice or blood.[45]

Then Paul says that "God did this (meaning to put forward Jesus as *hilasterion*) to show his righteousness." In a traditional understanding, "his righteousness" is understood as God's justice that requires a sacrifice to deal with sins. Likewise, Jesus's death is understood as necessary redemptive suffering to deal with sins, as shown in ransom theory, penal-substitution theory or in satisfaction theory. He was punished because of our sins, and his death satisfied God's justice, paying the debt of sins. The NIV follows this line of thought and translates 3:25–26 as follows: "God presented Christ as *a sacrifice of atonement*, through *the shedding* of his blood—*to be received* by faith. He did this to demonstrate his righteousness, because in his forbearance he had left the sins committed beforehand *unpunished*— he did it to demonstrate his righteousness at the present time, *so as to be just* and the one who justifies those who *have faith in Jesus*" (Italics are mine for emphasis). In this translation, the traditional atonement theory is confirmed further in the following: "God presented Jesus as a sacrifice of atonement through *the shedding* of his blood—*to be received* by faith (italics for emphasis)." Consistently, God did this "to demonstrate his righteousness" because he did not punish the sins committed beforehand. Here, we see the language of punishment of sins, and the implication is Jesus's

43. Stanley Stowers, *A Rereading of Romans*, 210.

44. Διὰ πίστεως (*dia pisteos*) means "through faith." This faith must be Jesus's faithfulness. See Bruce Longenecker, "ΠΙΣΤΙΣ in Romans 3:25: Neglected Evidence for the Faithfulness of Christ," 478–480. See also Charles Talbert, *Romans*, 107, 110. Talbert translates διὰ πίστεως Ἰησοῦ Χριστοῦ in 3:22 as "through his/Jesus' faithfulness" and ἐκ πίστεως Ἰησοῦ in 3:26 as "out of the faithfulness of Jesus." Richard Longenecker also comments that it is awkward to insert believer's faith along with Jesus's blood. To see it as God's faith is also an awkward idea because the main topic is Jesus and ἱλαστήριον. Moreover, there is no formulation like this in Paul's undisputed letters: "through faith in his blood." See Richard Longenecker, *The Epistle to the Romans*, 388–469.

45. Johnson, *Reading Romans*, 61. See also Richard Longenecker, *The Epistle to the Romans*, 388–469. Also, Charles Talbert, *Romans*, 107.

sacrifice is a punishment for the previous sins of humanity. So God is just because he does not allow the unpunished sins. God dealt with the former sins and now opens a new way of salvation and justification to be received by faith that Jesus's sacrifice is effective for all who believe. Namely, God justifies those who have faith in Jesus.[46]

But we can understand "God's righteousness" in 3:25 differently; namely, it can be understood as God's steadfast love and care for humanity. In other words, because of his Son's faithfulness and moral sacrifice, God decided to deal with the sins previously committed and opened a new path of reconciliation through faith that is based on Jesus's faithfulness. Jesus's faithfulness proved that God is righteous. Also, God is righteous because he dealt with all the past. Paul does not explicitly relate Jesus' death to the vicarious redemptive suffering of Jesus for the sins unpunished. In other words, there is hardly a sense that God requires his Son to be killed as a sin-offering.[47] Rather, Jesus' death is the result of his faithfulness to God. With this view of Jesus' death, Paul believes that God dealt with the sins previously committed (not "unpunished" as in the NIV) because of Jesus' faithfulness and his holy sacrifice. Namely, the past human history is mended because of Jesus's faithfulness. Therefore, in 3:26, but now, people must have the faithfulness of Jesus and live by it. 3:26 shows this emphasis: "It was to prove at the present time that he himself is righteous and that he justifies the one who has the faith of Jesus." God justifies those who share Jesus's faithfulness, which means changing their minds toward God and Christ. This idea is seen well in a chiasm in 3:21–26.

Chiasm in 3:21–26

A But now, apart from law, God's righteousness has been disclosed through Jesus's faithfulness for all who believe (v. 21–22)

    B All have sinned and fall short of the glory of God (v. 23)

---

46. Regarding the history of interpretation about "justification by faith," see Mark Reasoner, *Romans in Full Circle*, 23–41. See also Jouette B. Bassler, *Navigating Paul*, 23–33.

47. In the Deutero-Pauline letters, and Hebrews, the emphasis is on the forgiveness of sins; for example, Col 1:14; Heb 9:22. In Paul's undisputed letters, Paul never uses "the forgiveness of sins."

C They are now justified by his grace as a gift, through the redemption that is in Christ Jesus, whom God put forward as ἱλαστήριον (v. 24–25a)

B′ God dealt with the sins previously committed and showed his righteousness (v. 25b)

A′ At the present time it was to prove that God is righteous; God justifies those who share Jesus's faithfulness (v. 26).

A (v. 21–22) shows the importance of God's righteousness that has come through Jesus's faithfulness for all who have faith. B (v. 23) is a summary repetition of Rom 1:18—3:20 where the main problem was sin and the human unfaithfulness to God. C (v. 24–25a) reverses the condition of humanity in 3:23. That is, people are now justified by the grace of God, through the redemption that is in Christ Jesus. This redemption work of Jesus is the place to which they must come (3:25a). This place is ἱλαστήριον and its meaning is "a new place of reconciliation." B′ (v. 25b) confirms the solution to the problem of human sinfulness and unfaithfulness as expressed in B (v. 23); that is, God cleared up sinful impurity in the past because of Jesus's faithfulness. In this act of God, God's righteousness was demonstrated. That is the evidence of God's righteousness. A′ (v. 26) is an emphatic verse to A (v. 21–22) in the sense that the present act of God is emphasized. That is, God is still loving and righteous and justifies those who have the faithfulness of Jesus.

3:27–31 Justification by the Law of Faith, Not by the Works of the Law

3:27–28 By the Law of Faith, Not by theWorks of the Law

Therefore, no one can boast about anything because one's justification or reconciliation with God is by the grace of God, through the redemption that is in Christ Jesus, as we saw in 3:24–26. Here in 3:27–28 again, Paul accentuates the ground of faith that makes a person be justified before God. The concept of justification concerns his/her relationships with God; thus, it may be primarily ethical. In mainline Jewish tradition, as in the Hebrew Bible, there is no concept of forensic salvation. Furthermore, nowhere in his letters does Paul explicitly articulate such a concept. Rather, he quotes from Hab 2:4, saying that the righteous one will live by faith. His concern is how one may join the household of God and how he/she can maintain such membership in Christ. Likewise, his primary concern is not individualistic salvation but the salvation of all, both Jews and Gentiles. Christian membership is possible through God's grace that is found in Christ. Otherwise, Paul never suggests that salvation or justification is done once and for all from the perspective of forensic salvation. While Augustine and Luther consider righteousness a transferable privilege or status because of Christ, Habakkuk's concern is how to live by faith under any circumstances. The faithful person is the righteous one (1:17). Paul's position that a person is justified by faith apart from the works of the law (3:28). Here, he distinguishes faith from the works of the law about which we will see more in 3:31.

3:29–30 Since God is One, Both Jews and Gentiles Are Justified through the Same Faith

Paul has a monotheistic view of God. He asks rhetorical questions and answers them: "Or is God the God of Jews only? Is he not the God of Gentiles also? Yes, of Gentiles also" (3:29). God is the God of both Jews and Gentiles. He does not acknowledge other deities in the Greco-Roman world. While Jews claim God as their God alone who made a covenant through Abraham and gave the law through Moses, Paul argues that this God is for all, Jews and Gentiles. Therefore, God's love and righteousness must extend to all. His next logical argument is therefore in 3:30: "since God is one; and he will justify the circumcised on the ground of faith and the uncircumcised through that same faith." The same God has the same rule to apply to all, which is the ground of faith. God will justify both Jews (the circumcised) and Gentiles (the uncircumcised) on an equal basis of faith. Indeed, faith has been always the basis for one's right relationship with God. Abraham had faith in God (we will see about this in 4:1–25). Jesus also had faith in God, and his followers must continue to be faithful to God through him. Through faith, one can live righteously. Paul's point is, faith has been the consistent rule of God through history.

3:31 But the Law Cannot be Overthrown by Faith

But Paul warns those who think that the law is obsolete and that it is replaced by faith. Again he asks a question and answers it right away: "Do we then overthrow the law by this faith? By no means! On the contrary, we uphold the law" (3:31). It is very plausible for Paul to speak to an imaginative audience who thinks that Judaism is wrong and that the law is useless. They think faith is sufficient for their justification or salvation. This arrogance results in antinomianism or anti-Judaism. Some of them think that their salvation is done already and they do not care about even the ethical part of the law, resulting in lawlessness. Against this possible misunderstanding about faith, Paul vehemently rejects such a view, saying "by no means! On the contrary, we uphold the law" (3:31). Paul's gospel does not repeal the law because it is a gift of God given through Moses. The law can function well if it is understood well, providing moral guidance to Israelites. The law can be kept well through faith in God. Thus, he says the law must be upheld. As we will see in 4:1–25, the law has to be guided by faith, which rests on God's grace and his promise. The law's purpose is not to maintain a sectarian community or to judge others. It is about the love of God and the love of neighbor. Jesus fulfilled the law in this regard (c.f., 10:4).

4:1–25 Abraham as the Father of Faith for All, Jews and Gentiles

4:1–5 Abraham's Faith, Not His Works, Considered as Righteousness

Earlier in 3:21–31, Paul argues that God's righteousness has been disclosed through Jesus Christ's faithfulness and that God justifies those who have the faithfulness of Jesus. He also argues that both Jews and Gentiles may be justified through the same faith because God is the God of all. He distinguishes faith from the works of the law while upholding the law. Now in 4:1–25, he articulates further why faith precedes the law and why it is necessary to one's justification. For this purpose, he takes the example of Abraham and David. In 4:1–5, he illustrates Abraham's faith as a basis for his justification. His argument is that Abraham was justified by faith, not by works. He was called by God and heard God's good news and promise to him. He believed (trusted) God and walked with him through the ups and downs in his life. Abraham's faith in God was reckoned to him as righteousness (quotes from Gen 15:6). This faith is not a mere belief about God or his promise. Abraham's faith is trusting God, and because of his trust, he should take all responsibilities and risks during his life.

In fact, what comes first before Abraham's faith is God's calling. Even before Abraham had faith in God, God had called him and promised blessings to him. Without God's grace, he would not have received God's calling.[48] When he was called, Abraham did not hesitate but promptly responded to God. He left his house and village and moved to an unknown place with God's promise alone. This faith of Abraham is considered a good thing for God. Through faith, Abraham is entered into a good relationship with God. Otherwise, he did not earn God's favor to be called and blessed. Therefore, Paul states: "For if Abraham was justified by works, he has something to boast about, but not before God" (4:2). He goes on to say: "Now to one who works, wages are not reckoned as a gift but as something due." (4:4). Paul's point is that the very first thing humans have to recognize is God's grace or calling and then their response to God. This response is what faith is and it must be ongoing through one's entire life. That is what Abraham did to God. In this regard, faith means trusting God and walking with him. That also means faith comes with good works. In the Hebrew Bible, in general, faith is never understood as a belief or knowledge apart from works. Paul also never thinks of faith as separated from works. Faith without love is nothing (1 Cor 13). Paul's point is faith goes hand in hand with good works.

4:6–8 David's Testimony about God's Grace as a Gift

Interestingly, Paul takes David to drive home his thesis about God's grace first, as seen in 4:1–5. He refers to David, saying: "So also David speaks of the blessedness of those to whom God reckons righteousness apart from works" (4:6). His point is God's reckoning of righteousness is not by works but by his grace. As we saw in the case of Abraham, God's grace comes before Abraham's faith. Paul also quotes from LXX Psalm 32:1–2: "Blessed are those whose iniquities are forgiven, and whose sins are covered; blessed is the one against whom the Lord will not reckon sin" (4:7–8; from Psalm 32:1–2). His point is a blessed one will not sin against others. In other words, the grace of God does not exempt Jews from their ethical duty of caring for others. This implies that no one can say to others that there is no hope or future for them. Abraham was nobody before he was called. But because of God's grace and his calling, he became someone special. He trusted God and followed him through faithfulness all the way in his life. In David's Psalm too, this logic applies. God forgave Israelites by his grace; it is grace because they did not

---

48. Indeed, it would be impossible to explore Paul's theology without the grace of God, as he says in Gal 2:21, 1 Cor 1:4 and 15:10.

earn it. If there were no grace of God, it would be impossible for them to have a good relationship with God. In 4:7–8, Paul says God's grace prevails.[49] He also says similarly in 1 Cor 15:10: "But by the grace of God I am what I am, and his grace toward me has not been in vain" (c.f., Ps 31).

4:9–12 Righteousness through Abraham's Faith, Before His Circumcision

In 4:9, Paul asks a rhetorical question about God's blessing, which was explored in 4:1–8: "Is this blessedness, then, pronounced only on the circumcised, or also on the uncircumcised?" Answering this, he argues that God's blessings apply both to the circumcised (Jews) and the uncircumcised (Gentiles) through the same faith. Taking Abraham's faith in Gen 15:6 as an example, Paul explains why the circumcision is not a condition for Abraham's justification. He states that Abraham's justification occurred before his circumcision (4:10). His point is more than the timing of Abraham's justification before his circumcision. Rather, the real issue is how or why he was considered a good man, namely to be considered righteous. The reason is he trusted God. Because he was faithful to God, Abraham "received the sign of circumcision as a seal of the righteousness that he had by faith while he was still uncircumcised" (4:11; c.f., Gen 17:11). That is, the circumcision is "a seal of the righteousness" as a result of his faith. Even the circumcision is an expression of Abraham's faithfulness to God because he listened to him.

Then, Paul develops the next point that Abraham became the ancestor of both Jews and Gentiles through faith, not by circumcision.[50] He says: "The purpose was to make him the ancestor of all who believe without being circumcised and who thus have righteousness reckoned to them, and likewise the ancestor of the circumcised who are not only circumcised but who also follow the example of the faith that our ancestor Abraham had before he was circumcised" (4:11b–12). He makes sure that both Jews and Gentiles need the faith that Abraham had before he was circumcised (4:12).

---

49. Jewett, *Romans*, 316–17.

50. Philip Esler considers Abraham as "a prototype of group identity." See Philip Esler, *Conflict and Identity in Romans*, 155–170.

4:13–17 The Promise/Grace of God through Faith for All, the Adherents of the Law and Those Who Share the Faith of Abraham

In 4:13–17, Paul explains why faith precedes the law. His point is well stated in 4:13: "For the promise that he would inherit the world did not come to Abraham or to his descendants through the law but through the righteousness of faith." Here, "through the righteousness of faith" involves a Greek genitive case, which must be an attributive genitive in the sense that God's promise comes through a right relationship with God by faith. In other words, the promise is accepted by faith, which is the basis of a good relationship with God. Thus Paul says in 4:14: "If it is the adherents of the law who are to be the heirs, faith is null and the promise is void." While the law is nothing wrong, it should not function on its own without faith. If the law is absolutized at the sacrifice of faith, it brings wrath because it does not function properly (4:15). The law is about the love of God and the love of neighbor (c.f., Deut 6:4; Lev 19:18). The law without faith may be hollow or dangerous because it can be used to suppress others.

Then, in 4:16–17, Paul concludes that the promise of God comes through faith for all—the adherents of the law and those who share the faith of Abraham. Through faith, God's grace and his promise come "not only to the adherents of the law but also to those who share the faith of Abraham (for he is the father of all of us)" (4:16). Abraham becomes an icon of faith and all people can be hopeful through the same faith. God is trusted in all circumstances because he "gives life to the dead and calls into existence the things that do not exist" (4:17).

4:18–22 The Proof of Abraham's Faith

In 4:18–22, Paul specifies what kind of faith Abraham had. His faith echoes faith in Heb 11 where the keyword is hope or assurance about the future. When he heard the promise of God regarding his numerous descendants, he was about a hundred years old and Sarah was barren. Yet, he believed that promise and endured, as 4:20–21 says: "No distrust made him waver concerning the promise of God, but he grew strong in his faith as he gave glory to God, being fully convinced that God was able to do what he had promised." Abraham had a dream that he would become the father of many nations even if he does not see that reality now. Because of his ongoing faith in God, he had a good relationship with God, which is stated as follows: "Therefore his faith was reckoned to him as righteousness" (4:22).

4:23–25 Abraham's Case Applying to Followers of Jesus Who Believe in God

Now, Paul applies Abraham's faith story to all the followers of Jesus who believe in God. The God of Abraham is also the God of Jesus and all his followers. Thus he says: "Now the words, 'it was reckoned to him,' were written not for his sake alone, but for ours also" (4:23–24a). It is no question that Jesus was also faithful to God as we saw in 3:21–26. Through faithfulness, he proclaimed God's good news and his righteousness. Because of his faith in God, he was sacrificed by evil hands. But it is also a sign of his love of God. Thus God vindicated him and made him live (c.f., 2 Cor 13:4). God put forward him as a new place of reconciliation (3:25). Likewise, Jesus's followers need this same faith in God and must follow Christ's faithfulness. Then, "it will be reckoned to us who believe in him [God] who raised Jesus our Lord from the dead, who was handed over to death for our trespasses and was raised for our justification" (4:24–25). Here, Jesus's death can be understood as a moral sacrifice "for our trespasses." In other words, the reason is "we did not die or we were so self-centered." "For our trespasses" also implies that we were implicit participants in crucifying Jesus. Roman authority is also responsible for his death. In other words, Paul does not say that Jesus was punished and executed instead of sinners. His death is a moral sacrifice that shows his love of God and the world. Through Jesus's moral sacrifice and his faithfulness, his followers can have a right relationship with God. Thus in 4:25, Paul says Jesus "was raised for our justification."

5:1–21 NEW LIFE THROUGH CHRIST'S ACT OF RIGHTEOUSNESS

In 5:1–11, Paul talks about the benefit and implications of justification that comes through faith and this talk continues throughout Rom 5–8. In these chapters, main topics are new life in Christ and how it can be maintained.[51] In 5:12–21, referring back to the topics in Rom 1–4 such as faith, justification, sin, and the law, he emphasizes the excellence of Christ's faithfulness and his act of righteousness. Jesus's faithfulness is excellent because he disclosed

---

51. See *Romans*, 346; Johnson, *Reading Romans*, 83–99.

God's righteousness, without being defeated by sin. Then, in 6:1–23, Paul tackles sin's problem and argues that the only way to overcome sin is to die to it. That is, one should not be deceived by it. New life requires dying to sin, which means to die to sinful passions in the body. If one dies to the old self, he or she will be freed from sin and can live to God. Then, in 7:1–25, he talks about the law's problem and how to overcome it. While the law is holy, it can be used by sin. That is, sin uses the law and produces in people covetousness and passions. The way out of this problem is to follow the law of God, not the law of sin. Finally, in 8:1–39, he talks about a new life in the Holy Spirit. While the flesh seeks human will, the Spirit seeks God's will. One must put to death the deeds of the body to be led by the Spirit (8:17).

With the above preview of Rom 5–8, this section will focus on 5:1–21, which is divided into two parts: 5:1–11 and 5:12–21. In the former, the benefits and implications of justification are discussed and related to the work of Christ and God's love. Namely, those who share the faithfulness of Jesus have the following benefits and implications: peace with God; the hope of sharing the glory of God; worthwhile sufferings; assurance of God's love; and reconciliation with God. In all of this, Jesus's grace and God's love are essential. In other words, the benefits of a new life (justification) are possible because of Jesus's holy sacrifice and his grace, which confirms the love of God. Then, in 5:12–21, Paul explains why the human condition is difficult to overcome and presents a new way of Christ Jesus. In doing so, he juxtaposes Adam's sin with Jesus's obedience and his act of righteousness.

Outline of 5:1–21

5:1–11 The benefits and Implications of "Justification through Faith"

5:1–2 Peace with God and the Hope of Sharing the Glory of God

In 5:1, Paul makes a shift to the result of justification, as he says: "Therefore, since we are justified by faith." Thus far, his argument is that the gospel is "the power of God for salvation to everyone who has faith, to the Jew first and also to the Greek" (1:16) and that in the gospel "God's righteousness is revealed from faith to faith" (1:17). Namely, he took the pain to explain the gospel of faith, quoting from Hab 2:4: "The one who is righteous will live by faith." The benefits or implications of justification are as follows: peace with God and the hope of sharing the glory of God (5:1–2); worthwhile sufferings (5:3–5); assurance of God's love (5:6–9); reconciliation with God (5:10–11).

Peace with God is possible because one has a right relationship with God "by faith" (*ek pisteos*). Faith is the basis for making peace with God. If people were faithful to God, there would be no wrath of God. Wrath is caused by people who are wicked and suppress the truth (1:18). 2:5 also confirms the human-caused wrath: "But by your hard and impenitent heart you are storing up wrath for yourself on the day of wrath, when God's righteous judgment will be revealed." Those who patiently do good and "seek for glory and honor and immortality" will receive eternal life (2:7). But "for those who are self-seeking and who obey not the truth but wickedness, there will be wrath and fury" (2:8).

Indeed, peacemaking with God involves all aspects of human life, including relationships with other human beings.[52] This is why Paul exhorts Christians to make peace with others in and outside of the church, as he says in 12:17–20: "Do not repay anyone evil for evil, but take thought for what is noble in the sight of all. If it is possible, so far as it depends on you, live peaceably with all. Beloved, never avenge yourselves, but leave room for the wrath of God; . . . 'if your enemies are hungry, feed them; if they are thirsty, give them something to drink; for by doing this you will heap burning coals on their heads.'"

But he also believes that the ultimate peace and restoration of God's creation will happen in the future, as he expresses such an idea in 8:22–24: "We know that the whole creation has been groaning in labor pains until

---

52. Jewett, *Romans*, 349.

now; and not only the creation, but we ourselves, who have the first fruits of the Spirit, groan inwardly while we wait for adoption, the redemption of our bodies. For in hope we were saved. Now hope that is seen is not hope. For who hopes for what is seen?"

It must be noted that this peacemaking with God is accomplished or realized through Jesus Christ in the present: "we have peace with God through our Lord Jesus Christ."[53] Paul does not say that "we obtained peace with God when Jesus died." The verb here is the present tense ("we have"), which implies that peacemaking with God is not done once and for all but is realized continuously through Christ. That is, one must follow Christ and his faithfulness. Even though Jesus died in the past for the ungodly, his influence on Christians must continue so that they may be in peace with God. This is what Paul says: "through whom we have obtained access to this grace in which we stand." That is, Christians look back to the past events of Jesus's life and death, and through him, they received the grace of God.

In sum, peace comes from God and is given to "all God's beloved in Rome, who are called to be saints" (1:7). Peace is given as a result of doing good through faith (2:10). Peace-seeking faith must be based on the truth of God (3:17). This idea of peacemaking is explicit in 8:6: "To set the mind on the flesh is death, but to set the mind on the Spirit is life and peace." Also, peacemaking is for mutual upbuilding (14:19) and should be done by the Holy Spirit (14:17; 15:13). Then, the God of peace will be with them (15:33) and eventually, he "will shortly crush Satan under your feet" on the day of the Parousia (16:20). In addition, people of peace have the hope of sharing God's glory in the future (c.f., 8:21). Until the Parousia, they must maintain their faith with patience and by the Holy Spirit.[54] Moreover, their boasting in the hope of sharing the glory of God in the future must be balanced with boasting in sufferings too, which is the topic of 5:3-5.

5:3–5 Worthwhile Sufferings

Overall, Paul's view of time and salvation comes with the "already but not yet." Until the Parousia, sufferings are inevitable because the present world is under the power of sin. Christians are no exception to this reality even though they taste the power of God through faith. In fighting against sin, they may end up having unnecessary sufferings. For example, if they refuse

---

53. See Klaus Haacker, *The Theology of Paul's Letter to the Romans*, 45.

54. See Rom 4:18; 8:20–25; 12:14; 15:4, 12.

to participate in state rituals or emperor worship, they will be in trouble or persecuted. They will also suffer their social relationships with other people in society. Moreover, if they preach the good news of God, not that of Rome, they will be also in big trouble. In this sense of an unavoidable reality in the world, Roman Christians must be ready to deal with their sufferings (8:18; c.f., 2 Cor 1:5–7). Paul, however, does not seem to encourage mere sufferings to Roman Christians, as if suffering is itself good for them. State torture and evil acts are evil and bad. But if those sufferings due to the gospel proclamation are unavoidable, they must undergo the process of transformation. That is where Paul introduces a chain of character development in Rom 5:3–4: "suffering produces endurance (*hypomone* as steadfastness or perseverance), and endurance produces character (*dokime*), and character produces hope (*elpida*)." Suffering produces endurance and it is not comparable to the glory of God in the future (c.f., 12:12; 2 Cor 1:6; 6:4; Phil 1:29; 3:10). When suffering is inevitable due to the work of God, one has to know it is a necessary cost. Therefore, he/she must endure through the help of the Holy Spirit (c.f., 8:26–27). Then, endurance brings about the character (*dokime*) such as proof, testing, evidence, or value (c.f., 2 Cor 2:9; 13:3; Phil 2:22). This means that one has to show proof of good Christian after a period of endurance. For example, Paul writes to see whether the Corinthians are doing well: "I wrote for this reason: to test you and to know whether you are obedient in everything" (2 Cor 2:9; 13:3; Phil 2:22). Finally, character produces hope (*elpida*). Ultimately, without hope, nothing will be sustained. Good faith, endurance, and character will be in vain without hope. Hope sustains Christian faith. This hope is about the future. Whatever happens badly now to Roman Christians, they have to see hope coming on the way. For example, Paul says in 5:5 that this hope does not disappoint Christians, "because God's love has been poured into our hearts through the Holy Spirit that has been given to us." Namely, God's love supports the hope of Christians, and the Holy Spirit works with them (c.f., 9:1; 14:17; 15:13; 1 Thess 1:5–6). But eventually, Christian faith and all good works must be based on God's love and Jesus's grace.

5:6–9 Assurance of God's Love Confirmed through Christ's Dying for the Ungodly

In 5:6, Paul says: "While we were still weak, at the right time Christ died for the ungodly." It is important to understand what it means that Jesus

Christ died for the ungodly. Jesus died not for God but for the ungodly. More importantly, he died not for the righteous but for the ungodly. Someone may die for a good cause, for a righteous person or for God. But Jesus does not belong to that kind of "noble" death. Namely, he was not executed on the cross because of his religious beliefs about God. Maccabees fought against the Seleucid Empire and died for God. They tried to defend their holy tradition. They are martyrs who died for God. But Jesus was brought to trials and executed because of his advocacy for the sinners, the poor, and marginalized. This is what "Jesus died for the ungodly" means. In other words, "the ungodly" is a term for those who are labeled ungodly in society.

This kind of death for the ungodly is a revolutionary one that reverses the honor-and-shame culture in the Greco-Roman world where the weak serve elites and noble persons. From the perspective of the Greco-Roman culture, Jesus's death for the ungodly, meaning all kinds of "bad" people is unseen or nonsense. It may be even an object of ridicule. But for Paul, it is an act of Jesus's love and his grace toward the weak or the marginalized, who are outside the imperial benefits of salvation or protection. In other words, Jesus's death is proof of God's love for them because he did not spare his life to disclose God's righteousness. So, Paul talks about God's love in this way: "God proves his love for us in that while we still were sinners Christ died for us" (5:8). In this verse, we see a shift of the object of Christ's dying from "for the ungodly" in 5:6 to "for us." This first-person plural in the "while we still were sinners" relates to "the ungodly" stated in 5:6. This implies that the historic death of Jesus has an impact on Roman Christians during Paul's time. In other words, the cause and meaning of his death must be reflected upon again and again. His dying for the ungodly or sinners is a one-time event but its impact is not so. Therefore, "Jesus's dying for us" is not to be understood as a one-time substitutionary death that solves human problems or sins at one time.[55] Rather, it is a representational moral death that expresses his love of God and the world.

Now, interestingly, Paul states that Christ's dying for sinners (namely, the ungodly) is the proof of God's love. In order to understand this fact, we need to understand Paul's theology is God-centered. Namely, God is behind what Christ did. For example, Jesus's faithfulness and his moral sacrifice, as we saw in 3:21–26, moved God to act gracefully for people. God put forward Jesus as "a new place of reconciliation" because of his Son's love

---

55. Daniel Powers, *Salvation through Participation*, 108. See also Jewett, *Romans*, 362–64.

and faithfulness. Keck observes about this as follows: "Paul's theology in Romans is theocentric but christomorphic-focused on God as understood in light of Christ."[56] That is, God recognizes Jesus's grace and love for sinners and makes him a new place of reconciliation. Now is the new time that they have to turn to God through Jesus. Being challenged by Jesus's bold faith and death for the sinners, Christians must abide by his faithfulness.

5:10–11 Reconciliation with God through Christ's Death

In 5:10–11, Paul turns to the language of reconciliation with God to explain the benefits of justification through faith. Before coming to God through Jesus Christ, they were enemies of God. They sought their own power and glory, ignoring the weak and the poor. But now they were reconciled to God through the death of his Son. Here, again, the death of his Son echoes his moral sacrifice for God's righteousness. Reconciliation with God happens not because of Jesus's sinless sacrifice but because of their repentance due to his moral sacrifice and following of Christ in his footsteps. Because of the challenge of Jesus's faithfulness, his followers are expected to follow him. In this way, we can understand the language of reconciliation in 5:10: "We were reconciled to God through the death of his Son."

But this reconciliation is achieved not once and for all as if they were saved already. Rather, Paul's language of salvation is, on the one hand, they are saved (the present tense), and on the other hand, they will be saved (the future tense). Therefore, reconciliation or salvation must be experienced continuously by participating in Christ's faith. That is why Paul goes on to say in 5:10: "having been reconciled, will we be saved by his life." Since the ultimate salvation is yet to come, Christians must live "by his life." This wording must be very surprising to some Roman Christians partly because they may have thought that their salvation was done. More than that, they also may have thought that they were saved *by his death*.[57] But Paul says that they *will be saved by his life*. Here "life" (*zoe*) stands for what Jesus lived for and what he became now. The former all his faithful works, hardships, and existential struggles for God's righteousness. The latter includes his resurrection and exaltation, which are God's work (c.f., 2 Cor 13:4). In sum, "by his life" means to follow him and expect to have the hope of sharing the

56. Leander Keck, *Romans*, 141.

57. From a forensic salvation perspective, salvation needs Jesus's death as a sin-offering. But here, interestingly, Paul says they will be saved by his life (*zoe*).

glory of God (5:2). Then, they can thank God for their salvation through Jesus through whom they have received reconciliation (5:11).

5:12–21 New Life through Christ's Act of Righteousness

5:12–14 Sin's Work in the World and Adam's Sin

In 5:12, Paul talks about several things: sin's coming into the world through one man; death's coming through sin; and death's spreading to all because all have sinned. First, he merely states that "sin came into the world through one man." Otherwise, he does not talk about its origin because he does not know. His real concern is not so much about where sin came from but the reality that it came into the world through one man. This one man is Adam who participated in sin according to Gen 2. Adam is a representative of sinful humanity. Since Adam, sin has pervaded the world, invading all human sphere.

Second, Paul states that "death came through sin." When there was sin, there was also death, which is a metaphor for spiritual death or "a cosmic power" that reigns the sphere of darkness in the world.[58] Spiritual death means no communication or relationship between God and humanity. When Adam and Eve sinned, their punishment is spiritual death because they did not obey God (Gen 2:17). Thus far Paul's point is threefold: (1) Adam is a representative of fallen humanity; (2) sin came through him; (3) death came through sin.

Third, Paul states that "so death spread to all because all have sinned." Here, the logic is interesting. He does not say death spread to all because of Adam; rather, it spread to *all because all have sinned.* While sin and death came through one man, Adam, the spreading of death is because all have sinned. In other words, they cannot blame Adam for their death. In other words, the so-called original sin theory does not work with Paul.[59] Adam is responsible for his own disobedience and hence his death. He affected all humanity after him. Nevertheless, he cannot be blamed for all sins after him.

In 5:13, Paul states: "sin was indeed in the world before the law, but sin is not reckoned when there is no law." The first part of this verse is easy to understand because he said earlier that sin came into the world. This

58. Jewett, *Romans*, 377.

59. J. T. Kirby, "The Syntax of Romans 5:12: A Rhetorical Approach," 283–86.

coming of sin was obviously before the law. But the second part of the verse is not easy to understand because sin is related to the law. One way we can understand this relationship is through the law's conviction to those who do not keep it (c.f., 7:7). The other way to understand this relationship is more proper than the former. That is, sin seizes an opportunity in the commandment and produces in a person all kinds of covetousness (7:8). In other words, the problem is not the law per se but sin's power working in the person. Thus, Paul says: "Apart from the law sin lies dead" (7:8). Likewise, he continues to say: "I was once alive apart from the law, but when the commandment came, sin revived" (7:9). Eventually, he says about the law in 7:14: "For we know that the law is spiritual; but I am of the flesh, sold into slavery under sin."

In 5:14, Paul says: "Yet death exercised dominion from Adam to Moses," which is a period before the law came. This is because sin was in the world before the law, as he said in 5:13. As we know from here, Paul's real concern is not the law per se but sin's existence and its use of sinful passions in the body. This point will be explored throughout Rom 6–7.

5:15–17 The Free Gift in the Grace of the One Man, Jesus Christ

Sin and death are juxtaposed with "the grace of God and the free gift in the grace of the one man, Jesus Christ" (5:15). Sin and death came through the one man, Adam, and all have participated in sin. Now that situation is reversed by "the grace of God and the free gift in the grace of the one man, Jesus Christ." As we saw in 3:24, justification is made by the grace of God, through the redemption that is in Christ Jesus. Here in 5:15, we see the same logic that the new life comes through the grace of God and Jesus. "The free gift" in the grace of Jesus refers to all benefits bestowed to Christians because of Jesus's ministry, such as "the gift of salvation and the specific gifts of God's mercy and calling into his gratifying service."[60] This free gift is the result of Jesus's devoting his life to God and his disclosing God's righteousness.

In 5:16, Paul says: "And the free gift is not like the effect of the one man's sin. For the judgment following one trespass brought condemnation, but the free gift following many trespasses brings justification." The free gift of justification is unlike the effect of Adam's sin because it is rooted "in the grace of Jesus." This means that Jesus's grace and his work of redemption

---

60. Jewett, *Romans*, 381–2.

have enough power to change the course of death-ruling effect and move to justification. This fact is stated in 5:17: "If, because of the one man's trespass, death exercised dominion through that one, much more surely will those who receive the abundance of grace and the free gift of righteousness exercise dominion in life through the one man, Jesus Christ." Truly, because the one man's trespass, death exercised dominion through that one. But we should not be confused with the fact that "death spread to all because all have sinned" (5:12). Likewise, the logic about the one man, Jesus Christ, goes like this: Because of the one man's grace, "those who receive the abundance of grace and the free gift of righteousness exercise dominion in life through the one man." This implies that their exercise of dominion in life must come through the one man Jesus, who showed faithfulness to God.

5:18–19 One Man's Disobedience Versus the One Man's Act of Righteousness

In 5:18–19, Paul goes into detail about sin and righteousness and juxtaposes Adam's sin with Jesus's act of righteousness. He says in 5:18: "Therefore just as one man's trespass led to condemnation for all, so one man's act of righteousness leads to justification and life for all." Jesus's act of righteousness refers to 3:22: "God's righteousness has been disclosed through Jesus Christ's faithfulness." Jesus's faithfulness has been explored in 3:21–26. Because of his moral sacrifice and faithfulness for God's righteousness, God was impressed by him and decides to open a new path of reconciliation through him (3:25). In 5:19, Paul continues to talk about the importance of Jesus's faithfulness in comparison with Adam: "For just as by the one man's disobedience the many were made sinners, so by the one man's obedience the many will be made righteous." Jesus's obedience entails his entire life.[61] Therefore, those who follow Jesus must be also obedient to God, following his will and walking his walk. That is what Paul says: "So one man's act of righteousness leads to justification and life for all." When people participate in Jesus's act of righteousness, they *will be made righteous* (5:19). Justification or salvation is yet to be completed in the future.

---

61. Ibid., 386. See also Otto Michel, *Der Briefe an die Römer*, 191. Käsemann, *Romans*, 157; C.E.B Cranfield, *A Critical and Exegetical Commentary on the Epistle to the Romans*, Vol. 1, 291.

5:20–21 Grace Reverses Sin's Power, Leading to Eternal Life

In 5:20–21, Paul reiterates the power of grace leading to eternal life through Jesus Christ. He is optimistic about justification and eternal life because grace abounds all the more in the midst of multiplying trespasses. When he says "where sin increased, grace abounded all the more," he does not mean that grace needs more trespasses so that grace may become more effective or powerful. His point is grace is more powerful than sin and that it can overcome sin through Jesus Christ.[62] Grace exercises "dominion through Jesus Christ our Lord" (5:21). Then, those who are under the lordship of Jesus are justified and have eternal life. If sin exercises dominion in death, they are ruled by sin and condemned.

6:1–7:25 MAINTENANCE OF NEW LIFE: DYING TO SIN AND DYING TO THE LAW

In 5:1–21, Paul said that the benefits of justification through Jesus's faithfulness are great and that Christians must face sufferings because of their life in Christ. He also said that God's love was proved by his Son's grace and faithfulness. He also said that the grace of God and Jesus's act of righteousness are excellent, so that Adam's sin may be overcome. But at the same time, Paul does not underestimate the human condition that sin came into the world, exercising dominion in death. He recognizes the pervasiveness and devastating power of sin. Because of this concern about sin and the difficult human condition, in Rom 6–7, he deals with the problem of sin in relation to grace and the law. In 6:1–23, the issue is how to overcome sin. The solution is to die to sin. Dying to sin means to die to the old self that seeks fleshly passions. In 7:1–25, he deals with the law and the problem of sin. The law is holy, but the problem is in sin working in the flesh. The way out of this problem is to follow the law of God, not the law of sin.

Outline of 6:1–7:25

6:1–23   Maintenance of new life through dying to sin
   6:1–13   Should we continue in sin in order that grace may abound?
   6:1–5   We died with Christ (baptism into his death)

---

62. Johnson, *Reading Romans*, 83.

6:1–23 Maintenance of New Life through Dying to Sin

6:1–13 Should We Continue in Sin in Order That Grace May Abound?

6:1–5 We Died with Christ ("baptism into his death")

In 6:1–2, Paul talks to an imaginary audience and asks rhetorical questions: "What then are we to say? Should we continue in sin in order that grace may abound?" These questions are raised in response to 5:20: "But law came in, with the result that the trespass multiplied; but where sin increased, grace abounded all the more." His answer is "by no means!" That is, Christians should not continue in sin because of grace. He goes on to ask: "How can we who died to sin go on living in it? Do you not know that all of us who have been baptized into Christ Jesus were baptized into his death?" (6:2–3). They cannot continue in sin even when grace abounds because they died to sin (the past tense), meaning to have died with Christ. What does it mean to die to sin and to die with Christ? First, since sin is power, to die to sin means to let sin not exercise dominion in our bodies. As Paul recognizes, sin came into the world, exercising dominion in death (5:12–21). It cannot be removed from the world until the very last when Jesus delivers the kingdom to God (1 Cor 15:20–28). The way to stop sin's power is to die to sin. This means Christians have to "put to death the deeds of the body by the Spirit" (8:13).

Second, with this view of "to die to sin" in mind, dying with Christ means to participate in his moral sacrifice and his faithfulness to God's righteousness. As we have seen in the previous chapters, Jesus followed God's will and was faithful to him, proclaiming God's good news and manifesting his righteousness. Because of his faithfulness to God's righteousness, he was sacrificed. So, dying with Christ means to follow his footsteps, risking one's life.

But Paul also reminds them that dying with Christ is not itself the goal. Rather, the goal is to walk in newness of life: "Therefore we have been buried with him by baptism into death, so that, just as Christ was raised from the dead by the glory of the Father, so we too might walk in newness of life" (6:4). Without dying with Christ, that is, without participating in his faithfulness, it is impossible to live the new life in him. Justification through faith needs ongoing participation in his faithfulness.[63] Then there will be an ultimate victory of new life on the Parousia: "For if we have been united with him in a death like his, we will certainly be united with him in a resurrection like his" (6:5).

6:6–8 THROUGH DYING OF OUR OLD SELF, THE BODY OF SIN MIGHT BE DESTROYED

Paul continues to talk about the implication of "dying with Christ" in 6:6–8: "We know that our old self was crucified with him so that the body of sin might be destroyed, and we might no longer be enslaved to sin. For whoever has died is freed from sin. But if we have died with Christ, we believe that we will also live with him." When one was crucified with Christ (the past tense), meaning to follow him and participate in his faithfulness, "the body of sin" is destroyed (the present tense). Dying with Christ precedes the destruction of "the body of sin," which means "the sinful or sin-ruled body" (an attributive genitive). In other words, if there is no dying with Christ, sin exercises dominion in the body through sinful passions (c.f., 5:20; 6:12; 7:5, 11). Therefore, the way of freedom from sin is to die with Christ, as it is stated in 6:7: "For whoever has died is freed from sin." Likewise, the way of life is through dying with Christ, as in Rom 6:8: "But if we have died with Christ, we believe that we will also live with him."

---

63. Jewett, *Romans*, 402; see also Robert Tannehill, *Dying and Rising with Christ*, 12.

6:9–10 CHRIST ALSO DIED TO SIN AND LIVES TO GOD

In 6:9–10, once again, Paul emphasizes Christ's dying to sin and his new life in God: "We know that Christ, being raised from the dead, will never die again; death no longer has dominion over him. The death he died, he died to sin, once for all; but the life he lives, he lives to God." Because of Jesus's faithfulness for God's righteousness, God raised him from the dead. He lives to God and will never die again. Likewise, "death no longer has dominion over him" because he "died to sin, once and for all." This means he did not let sin exercise in his body by keeping faith in God and following his will. He was crucified because of this, but God made him live. Paul gives us a hint about this new life of Jesus from 2 Cor 13:4: "For he was crucified in weakness, but lives by the power of God."

6:11–13 DO NOT LET SIN EXERCISE DOMINION IN OUR BODIES

In 6:11, Paul asks Christians to do the same thing with Christ: to die to sin and live to God in Christ Jesus: "So you also must consider yourselves dead to sin and alive to God in Christ Jesus." If they die to sin, sin will not exercise dominion in their bodies. Then, they have to overcome the passions of the body (6:12). In 6:13, Paul specifies how to overcome sin regarding the body: "No longer present your members to sin as instruments of wickedness, but present yourselves to God as those who have been brought from death to life, and present your members to God as instruments of righteousness." In this verse, "your members" are body parts (*mele*) such as hands or legs,[64] which should not be used for sin as instruments of wickedness. In other words, each person must present the whole person to God, which also means presenting his/her body parts to God as instruments of righteousness. The whole person with whole body parts must be for God and his righteousness. Paul claims that the body is for God and that it is not worthless. His view differs from some in the Corinthian church who argue that the body is nothing. They say they are free in Christ and they can do anything. But Paul warns them in 1 Cor 6:15–20. Here, Paul asks the Corinthians to use body parts responsibly so that they may glorify God in their body. Their bodies are not theirs and more importantly, the body is a temple of the Holy Spirit. At the same time, their bodies are parts (*mele*)

---

64. Jewett, *Romans*, 408–410.

of Christ; that is, metaphorically, they constitute body parts of Christ. This means they have to embody Christ in their lives.

6:14–18 Should We Sin Because We are Not under Law But under Grace?

Earlier in 6:1–3, Paul raised questions about sin and abundant grace. That is, the primary question is whether Christians can continue in sin in order that grace may abound. His answer is "by no means!" They should not continue in sin because they died to it. Then sin will not exercise dominion in their mortal bodies. But once again, he says similar things in 6:14–15: "For sin will have no dominion over you, since you are not under law but under grace. What then? Should we sin because we are not under law but under grace? By no means!" Their freedom is not for sin. They are not freed from sin once and for all. Indeed, they have a choice between slaves of sin and slaves of righteousness. The former means one's living by sinful passions, but the latter means one's commitment to living by obedience to God or his righteousness. No one can stay in between them. One is either a slave of sin or a slave of righteousness. While sin leads to death, obedience leads to righteousness (6:16). In 6:17, Paul says Christians changed their identity from slaves of sin to slaves of righteousness. "Slaves of righteousness" means they have to live for and by God's righteousness. As God's righteousness has been disclosed through Jesus Christ's faithfulness, all those who follow Jesus must demonstrate God's righteousness.

6:19–23 The Advantage of Being Enslaved to God: Sanctification and Eternal life

In 6:19, Paul says: "I am speaking in human terms because of your natural limitations. For just as you once presented your members as slaves to impurity and to greater and greater iniquity, so now present your members as slaves to righteousness for sanctification." In this verse, Paul emphasizes the importance of sanctification. Now Christians have to present their body parts to God and his righteousness. Then they can be sanctified. Sanctification requires a separation from the life of sin and death (6:20–23). The end of sanctification is eternal life in Christ Jesus (6:22–23).

7:1–25 Maintenance of New Life through Dying to the Law

7:1–6 Dying to the Law through "the Body of Christ"

In 7:1, Paul asks a question about the law and addresses the mixed community of Jews and Gentiles: "Do you not know, brothers and sisters—for I am speaking to those who know the law—that the law is binding on a person only during that person's lifetime?" He argues that the law's time ended and that they are free from it (7:2–3). The reason is stated in 7:4: "In the same way, my friends, you have died to the law through the body of Christ, so that you may belong to another, to him who has been raised from the dead in order that we may bear fruit for God." Here, the key interpretive issue is about "dying to the law through the body of Christ." What does Paul mean? Does the law refer to the Torah in general or specific laws? What is the body of Christ here? He does not seem to refer to the Torah because it is holy (7:12). But he refers to the specific use or function of the law, as indicated in 7:6: "But now we are discharged from the law, dead to that which held us captive, so that we are slaves not under the old written code but in the new life of the Spirit." He refers to the law that "held us captive." In other words, the law can function negatively if it is misinterpreted or not practiced properly because of sinful passions.[65] In this sense, the real issue is rather the human problem of sinful passions and the law is itself neutral. Paul explains this very well in 7:5: "While we were living in the flesh, our sinful passions, aroused by the law, were at work in our members to bear fruit for death" (c.f., 7:8). He goes on to say in 7:6: "But now we are discharged from the law, dead to that which held us captive, so that we are slaves not under the old written code but in the new life of the Spirit."

With the above clarification of the law, "our dying to the law" means the law does not exercise dominion in our bodies because we do not live in the flesh, with our sinful passions, aroused by the law (7:5). Later in 8:13, Paul says clearly about this: "for if you live according to the flesh, you will die; but if by the Spirit you put to death the deeds of the body, you will live." In a way, as we saw in Rom 6, the real problem is sin that uses the law. This discussion about sin and its use of the law continues throughout Rom 7. While sin is blamed for all evil, people are responsible for their actions. This means they must control their sinful passions aroused by the law.

---

65. The problem of the law occurs when some Jews have a zeal for God, as Paul says in Rom 10:2: "I can testify that they have a zeal for God, but it is not enlightened" (see also Gal 1:13–14; Phil 3:6).

Otherwise, "dying to the law" does not mean that they (Christians) are free from the law in the sense that the law ceases to function or because faith or Jesus replaced it. In 3:31, the law cannot be nullified by faith; rather, it must be upheld. What they are dead to is that which held them captive— the particular function of the law that works with sin and human passions. In 7:6, "dying to the law" means "we are slaves not under the old written code," which represents a narrow interpretation of the law because of our sinful passions or zeal for God. Now they have to live in the new life of the Spirit. In order to live the new life in the Spirit, the law must be interpreted and practiced through the lens of faith as we saw in 3:27–31 and Rom 4. What comes first is God's promise (or grace) and then faith comes (Rom 4). Faith is followed by the law. The former informs the latter of which the focus is the love of God and the love of neighbor. The law cannot prevent God's universal, impartial love from spreading to all peoples. It is Paul's understanding that the Abrahamic covenant extends to all regardless of who they are. That is, God's mercy and justice go beyond law-absolutism and Jewish ethnocentrism. Jesus is the example that he showed the purpose of the law and fulfilled it in his work, as 10:4 implies: "For Christ is the goal (*telos*) of the law so that there may be righteousness for everyone who believes." The law's purpose is "righteousness for everyone who has faith," which means their new life in Christ. Paul believes that Christ fulfilled the law through faith and disclosed God's righteousness to the world (3:22; 10:4). More than this, he also believes that Jesus is the Messiah (Christ) and the Son of God through whom God's new time dawned on humanity (3:21–26); as a result, Christians can live in the new life of the Spirit (7:6).

Regarding "the body of Christ," Paul says: "You have died to the law through the body of Christ" (7:4). "The body of Christ" is a genitive case that is difficult to understand. One plausible interpretation is it denotes Christ's crucifixion.[66] But what is the precise relation between "dying to the law" and "through Christ's crucifixion"? In Paul's view, Jesus died to sin (6:10) and also died to the law in a particular context as we saw before. Namely, 7:6 implies that Jesus was a slave not "under the old written code but in the new life of the Spirit." Likewise, Christians also died to the captive use of the law just as Jesus did.

---

66. Jewett, *Romans*, 433–34. See also Kim, *A Theological Introduction to Paul's Letters*, 83–108. But alternatively, we can also understand "the body of Christ" as an attributive genitive: "Christ-like body." Then, we can translate Rom 7:4 differently: "You have died to the captive use of law through Christ-like life—that is, through the way Christ has lived."

7:7–13 The Law is Not Sin; the Problem is Sin

Turning back to the issue of the law and sin, Paul again raises a rhetorical question to his audience: "What then should we say? That the law is sin?" (7:7). He distinguishes between the law and sin. The law is not itself sin, as he answers: "By no means!" (7:7). The law helps people understand what is wrong and what is right. Through the law, sin is exposed clearly: "Yet, if it had not been for the law, I would not have known sin. I would not have known what it is to covet if the law had not said, 'You shall not covet'" (7:7). From his context, Paul only focuses on this function of the law that reveals sin. Otherwise, he does not say that the law is wrong, inferior, or imperfect, or that the law is sin. Rather, "the law is holy, and the commandment is holy and just and good" (7:12). Having said this, he now goes on to discuss sin's problem and its relation to the law. The problem is sin that seizes "an opportunity in the commandment, produced in me all kinds of covetousness" (7:8). If sin works in the law, producing in a person the sinful passions (c.f., 7:5), there is little hope to get out of it unless he/she dies to it. So, "apart from the law sin lies dead" in 7:8 must be understood from this view that as long as sin is alive in the law, the stake is high. This is because sin does not give up on the law, as Paul says: "I was once alive apart from the law, but when the commandment came, sin revived" (7:9). This is not because the law is evil but because sin, "seizing an opportunity in the commandment, deceived me and through it killed me" (7:11). Once again, Paul makes sure about the law in 7:13: "Did what is good, then, bring death to me? By no means! It was sin, working death in me through what is good, in order that sin might be shown to be sin, and through the commandment might become sinful beyond measure."

7:14–25 The Law is Spiritual; A Realistic Struggle between the Law of God and the Law of Sin

In 7:14, Paul says: "The law is spiritual (*pneumatikos*); but I am of the flesh, sold into slavery under sin." That the law is spiritual connotes several things. First, the law or "the Torah was created, activated and authorized by the Spirit."[67] Therefore, the law must be holy (7:12). Second, that the law is spiritual can be understood as the law seeking spiritual matters or matters of the Spirit, beyond earthly things or flesh desires on earth. Christians are

---

67. Jewett, *Romans*, 461.

caught up in between seeking the law of the Spirit and the law of sin. Thus Paul says: "but I am of the flesh, sold into slavery under sin" (7:14). His point is that he cannot avoid a constant fight against the temptation of sin and flesh. That is, nothing has been resolved about sin other than fighting against it. This struggle between the matters of the spirit and matters of the flesh is well stated in 7:15-21. Here, however, Paul does not limit his discussion to an individual existential struggle between the spirit and the flesh, but his emphasis is simply that sin is too powerful to be completely defeated at once.[68] It is everywhere in the world and seizes an opportunity in the law to deceive a person. Paul does not underestimate the power of sin working everywhere and taking every opportunity to deceive a person. Sin is named and blamed for, but that does not mean Christians are not responsible for their evil deeds.

In 7:22-25, Paul concludes this ongoing fight between the spirit and the flesh.[69] On the one hand, he says in 7:22: "For I delight in the law of God in my inmost self." This means he can do his best without feeling guilty about his imperfection. But on the other hand, he faces a serious reality that he sees another law of sin within him (7:23). However, his view of the flesh is not the same as the Hellenistic dualism. He does not denigrate the body or flesh. The only problem with the body or flesh is it is weak and susceptible to the power of sin.

In 7:24, Paul laments: "Wretched man that I am! Who will rescue me from this body of death?" When he looks into himself, he has despair that he cannot overcome "this body of death," which means that death or sin rules the body (c.f., "the sinful body in 6:6). But he gives thanks to God through Jesus Christ in 7:25, saying that "with my mind I am a slave to the law of God, but with my flesh I am a slave to the law of sin." Here, "a slave to the law of God" echoes "slaves of righteousness" in 6:15-18 whereas "a slave to the law of sin" echoes "slaves of sin." This statement in 7:25 leaves a double entendre in ways that on the one hand, one can follow God through the mind, but on the other hand, one is still under the power of sin because of the flesh. This issue of the ongoing fight between the mind and the flesh continues in Rom 8. For example, 8:5-6 reads: "For those who live according to the flesh set their minds on the things of the flesh, but those who live

68. Wasserman's proposal must be helpful in that she argues that "I" in Rom 7 can be understood as "the death of the soul" or human immorality rooted in human disobedience in Rom 1:18-32. Emma Wasserman, *The Death of the Soul in Romans 7*.

69. See Craig Keener, *Romans*, 95-97.

according to the Spirit set their minds on the things of the Spirit. To set the mind on the flesh is death, but to set the mind on the Spirit is life and peace."

8:1–39 NEW LIFE IN THE SPIRIT

In Rom 5–7, Paul assured Roman Christians about the benefits of new life because of God's grace and Jesus's act of righteousness that reverse sin's work. He also explained how the new life in the Spirit can be maintained in spite of the difficult human condition that sin came into the world. That is, sin is pervasive and dwells in human minds and hearts. The way out of sin is to die to it, which means overcoming sinful passions. After a long discussion about the maintenance of new life of the Spirit, Paul concludes in Rom 8 that Christians are not condemned anymore because they are in Jesus and that they have to live by the Spirit. Here, the point is that those who are in Christ (*en christo*), that is, those who share his faithfulness, will not be condemned because they follow the law of faith, not the law of sin. Jesus died to sin and lives to God. Therefore, Christians also need to follow him and walk according to the Spirit, not according to the flesh. The above points are argued well with a chiasm in Rom 8.

Overall, in Rom 8, Paul emphasizes the power and role of the Spirit, which sustains God's ongoing work of salvation through Christ, and at the same time empowers Christians to stay in faith.[70] The Spirit is the power that reverses sin's power. Jesus overcame sin's power through the Spirit of God. Now both the Spirit of God and the Spirit of Christ dwell in Roman Christians (or simply children of God); therefore, they must live according to the Spirit, which means several things: "putting to death the deeds of the body" (8:13) and allowing for the Spirit's role in Christian life, as stated in 8:14–27, in particular. The Spirit sustains Christian life until the end. It also helps them in their weakness and intercedes for them in all situations.

Rom 8 is also a transition chapter to Rom 9–11 in which Paul extends the power of the gospel to Israel. Before going there, he assures Roman Christians about God's love in Christ Jesus and the help of the Spirit in their lives. He encourages them to stay in the Spirit by living according to it, reminding them of the ultimate victory in God: "the creation itself will be set free from its bondage to decay and will obtain the freedom of the glory of the children of God . . . and not only the creation, but we ourselves, who

70. Keck, *Romans*, 218.

have the first fruits of the Spirit, groan inwardly while we wait for adoption, the redemption of our bodies" (8:21–23). But from his Jewish perspective, what is missing in the above description of the ultimate victory in the gospel of God is the destiny of Israel or Jews. Some of the urgent questions lurking in his mind would be: "Does God not care about Jews who do not accept and follow Jesus as the Messiah? Does God nullify the Abrahamic covenant with his descendants? Is Israel excluded from participating in the final redemption of the bodies because of their unfaithfulness? What would be the destiny of unfaithful Jews?" These topics will be dealt with in Rom 9–11, which are essential chapters to Romans; they are not straw or unnecessary chapters. Paul's gospel of faith does not need to reject the law or Israel. Rather, it needs Israel because God is faithful. While faith is important to justification, the law is not itself the problem. The real problem is sin and the crooked human heart. Ultimately, it is God who will work out the salvation of Israel according to his time plan. That is Paul's thinking about Jews. In fact, Paul already partially dealt with the questions about the law and Israel in Rom 1–8, but he did not fully explore about them. For example, in 3:1–3: "Then what advantage has the Jew? Or what is the value of circumcision? Much, in every way. For in the first place the Jews were entrusted with the oracles of God. What if some were unfaithful? Will their faithlessness nullify the faithfulness of God?" The answer to this last question is "by no means!" Likewise, he confirms the holiness of the law (7:2) and never directly disputes the place of Israel because of faith. His position is that God is for all and that Jesus showed his righteousness through faith; therefore, all can become children of God through the same faith regardless of who they are. Yet, he cannot pass on the questions about Israel or Jews in his gospel. He asks related Jewish questions in his gospel, as in 11:1–2: "I ask, then, has God rejected his people? By no means! I myself am an Israelite, a descendant of Abraham, a member of the tribe of Benjamin. God has not rejected his people whom he foreknew. Do you not know what the scripture says of Elijah, how he pleads with God against Israel?" (11:1–2).

Outline of Rom 8:1–39

A 8:1–4 Assurance of new life in Christ Jesus

    B 8:5–11 New life by the Spirit of God and of Jesus, not by the flesh

    C 8:12–13 By the Spirit put to death the deeds of the body,
      then you will live
  B 8:14–27 The role of the Spirit of God for children of God
A 8:28–39 Assurance of the love of God in Christ

A, 8:1–4 Assurance of New Life in Christ

8:1–4 constitutes a chiasmus A that shows the assurance of new life in Christ Jesus. Paul states in 8:1: "There is therefore now no condemnation for those who are in Christ Jesus." This assurance concludes all he has talked throughout Rom 1–7. That is, the power of the gospel is excellent and secured in Christ. God's gospel is for everyone and does not discriminate against any conditions of a person. The gospel is the power of God for everyone who has faith (1:16–17). Therefore, those who come to God through Jesus can experience the power of God. "Those who are in Christ Jesus" means those who share the faithfulness of Jesus, as we saw in 3:26: "It was to prove *at the present time* that he himself is righteous and that he justifies the one *who shares the faithfulness of Jesus.* As we see above, 8:1 shows a recurrent theme that new life in Christ needs faith and participation.

In 8:2, Paul reminds Roman Christians how this new life in Christ happened: "For the law of the Spirit of life in Christ Jesus has set you free from the law of sin and of death."[71] "The law of sin" means to live according to sinful passions (6:12). It also means that people present their body parts (*mele*) to sin "as instruments of wickedness" (6:13). Likewise, "the law of death" means similar to "the law of sin" in the sense that death rules life (c.f., 5:12–14). Here death is "a cosmic power" that reigns the sphere of darkness in the world.[72] From "this law of sin and of death," Christians have been freed and "enslaved to God" (6:22). To clarify, Paul never meant that they were completely freed from sin once and for all, but they were freed from "the law of sin." Otherwise, sin is power that cannot be removed from the world until the Parousia. Only when people die to sin, they can walk in newness of life (6:4).

This newness of life comes from "the law of the Spirit of life in Christ Jesus" (8:2), which makes possible Christian freedom "from the law of sin

---

71. Here, "the law" does not refer to the Torah or Jewish laws. It means rule or principle, as in the law of faith (Rom 3:27). For more about this issue, see Jewett, *Romans*, 480–82; Keck, *Romans*, 196–7; Johnson, *Reading Romans*, 128.

72. Jewett, *Romans*, 377.

and of death." "The law of the Spirit" means to live according to the Spirit (8:4–6), which is explained in the ensuing verses. It also means to submit to "the law of God" (7:22) and to present body parts (*mele*) as "instruments of righteousness" (6:13).

This law of the Spirit leads to life. So Paul says: "The law of the Spirit of life in Christ Jesus set us free . . . ." Life is the opposite of death, which comes from sin (c.f., 5:12). "The law of the Spirit of life" is connected with "in Christ Jesus," which is a modal dative that points to the way Christ lived. This means the new life of the Spirit depends on Christ's work and his faithfulness. That is, Jesus showed history-changing examples of freedom from sin when he died to sin: "The death he died, he died to sin, once for all; but the life he lives, he lives to God" (6:10).[73]

In 8:3–4, Paul explains what God and Jesus have done to make this freedom of new life possible: "For God has done what the law, weakened by the flesh, could not do: by sending his own Son in the likeness of sinful flesh, and to deal with sin, he condemned sin in the flesh, so that the just requirement of the law might be fulfilled in us, who walk not according to the flesh but according to the Spirit." Paul believes that God sent his Son to deal with and condemn sin. Sin was condemned through Jesus's faithful work and moral sacrifice for God's righteousness. Sin tried to win Jesus, but he did not submit to the law of sin but submitted to God's law. He became instruments of righteousness. Ironically, because of his faithful work for God, he was crucified. But sin is condemned on his cross because God judges evil. Sin never fully exercised dominion on Jesus because he died to it. So sin was condemned in the flesh, which means Jesus's own life and the world. Paul does not say that Jesus's death removed sin, but it was condemned because of Jesus's work and faithfulness to God.

This sin refers to our early discussion in Rom 6–7. That is, since sin is power and pervasive, it cannot be removed by Jesus's death. He won the fight against sin. This is what "For God has done what the law, weakened by the flesh, could not do" means. "The just requirement of the law" (8:4) nails down to the love of neighbor, as stated later in 13:8–10: "Owe no one anything, except to love one another; for the one who loves another has fulfilled the law. The commandments, 'You shall not commit adultery; You shall not murder; You shall not steal; You shall not covet'; and any other commandment, are summed up in this word, 'Love your neighbor as

---

73. Here Jesus's living to God echoes "a life-giving spirit" in 1 Cor 15:45. See Johnson, "Life-Giving Spirit: The Ontological Implications of Resurrection," 75–89.

yourself." Love does no wrong to a neighbor; therefore, love is the fulfilling of the law" (c.f., Gal 5:14). Because Jesus fulfilled the law, Christians need to follow his faithfulness and "walk not according to the flesh but according to the Spirit" (8:4).

B, 8:5–11 New Life by the Spirit of God and of Jesus, Not by the Flesh

8:5–8 constitutes a chiasmus B that contrasts two different ways of life: to live according to the flesh and to live according to the Spirit. Paul asks Roman Christians to choose life by the Spirit of God and of Jesus Christ. Flesh (*sarx*) appears ten times in Rom 8 alone and spirit (*pneuma*) appears a lot more times here, nineteen times. To live according to the flesh means they set their minds on the things of the flesh, which means to seek fleshly passions. Those who live this way leads to death (8:6), which connotes a spiritual death or a status under the control of sin and death (c.f., 5:12–14). Otherwise, the flesh is not itself wrong. On the contrary, to live according to the Spirit means to set their minds on the things of the Spirit, which means to seek matters of the Spirit or God's righteousness. The result is life and peace (8:7). As Jesus manifested God's righteousness through faithfulness, his followers have to do the same through faith. Then there will be abundant life and peace. But those who seek their own power and glory are hostile to God because they do not submit to God's law (8:7), which means to submit to God and to seek God's will.

Contrasting a life by the flesh and life by the Spirit, he exhorts Roman Christians to live in or by the Spirit of God and of Jesus (8:9–11). He reminds them of their ethical identity in the Spirit. In 8:9, he says: "But you are not in the flesh; you are in the Spirit." While they live in the flesh, their goal is not to seek fleshly things such as fame or power. Rather, they are in the Spirit, which means that they think and behave in view of what the Spirit wants. But this Spirit is not alone at work. Paul provides the reason why they are in the Spirit: "Since the Spirit of God dwells in you" (8:9; c.f., 1 Cor 6:19–20). The Spirit is none other than the Spirit of God.[74] In other words, the Spirit comes from God and does not work independently. It is sent by God and works for him. This Spirit of God also dwells in Roman

---

74. The idea about the Spirit of God comes from 1 Cor 2:11: "For what human being knows what is truly human except the human spirit that is within? So also no one comprehends what is truly God's except the Spirit of God."

Christians. Therefore, they must depend on the Spirit in their works for God.

Then Paul adds another sentence to this: "Anyone who does not have the Spirit of Christ does not belong to him" (8:9). "The Spirit of Christ" is the same as earthly Jesus. The former means "a life-giving spirit" after God's raising of Jesus from the dead, as 1 Cor 15:45 puts as follows: "The first man, Adam, became a living being; the last Adam became a life-giving spirit." The last Adam is Jesus Christ who was raised from the dead; he became a spirit that gives life. This implies that the risen Lord continues to help his followers to live in abundance of life and peace. If this Spirit of Jesus is in them, they can live a life of peace and righteousness because they may overcome the power of sin (8:10). Paul's point is Roman Christians are under the lordship of Christ. They must know how he lived faithfully for God's righteousness with the lead of the Spirit of God. With the above explanation, 8:9b is understandable better: "Anyone who does not have the Spirit of Christ does not belong to him." If the Spirit of Christ does not dwell in them, they do not belong to Christ. Mere membership in Christ or in the Church does not help. They need the lordship of Christ in everyday life.

Lastly, in 8:11, once again, Paul stresses the role and work of the Spirit of God. That is, if the Spirit of God dwells in them, God who raised Christ from the dead will give life to their mortal bodies through his Spirit that dwells in them.

C, 8:12–13 By the Spirit Put to Death the Deeds of the Body, Then You Will Live

8:12–13 constitutes a chiasmus C that shows the importance of the practice of living by the Spirit. If the Spirit of God dwells in Christians, they have to "put to death the deeds of the body by the Spirit" (8:13; c.f., 6:6–10; 7:4–5). In other words, they have to depend on the Spirit and make efforts to control their sinful passions. They cannot win the fight against sinful passions. The Spirit of God should help them in all circumstances. But there must be also human efforts of putting to death the deeds of the body. When they do so, they will live. Note here the future tense of "to live." If they live according to the flesh, they will die (8:13). Salvation is yet to complete.

B, 8:14–27 The Role of the Spirit of God for Children of God

8:14–27 constitutes a chiasmus *B* that explains the role of the Spirit of God for children of God. In this section, Paul makes sure about the Spirit of God that helps them in their weakness, in fact, in all circumstances. In 8:14, he says that "all who are led by the Spirit of God are children of God." In other words, if they are not led by the Spirit of God, they are not called "children of God." Using a metaphor of slavery and adoption, Paul ensures about their new life to be led by the Spirit: "For you did not receive a spirit of slavery to fall back into fear, but you have received a spirit of adoption. When we cry, 'Abba! Father!' it is that very Spirit bearing witness with our spirit that we are children of God" (8:15–16). They are not orphaned even after Jesus is gone because the Spirit helps them in their weakness and "intercedes with sighs too deep for words" and according to the will of God (8:25–27).

If they are children of God being led by the Spirit, they must suffer with Christ so that they may "also be glorified with him" (8:17). The idea that dying with Christ and gaining a new life is one of the most salient themes in Romans (for example 6:3–5). Paul never claims that Christ did everything for salvation and that Christians' job is to believe in him. Rather, the point is newness of life comes from dying with Christ. He also says similarly in 5:3–5: "And not only that, but we also boast in our sufferings, knowing that suffering produces endurance, and endurance produces character, and character produces hope, and hope does not disappoint us, because God's love has been poured into our hearts through the Holy Spirit that has been given to us." In the end, the whole creation will be restored from suffering (8:19–23).

In 8:19, Paul says that "the creation waits with eager longing for the revealing of the children of God." Here, he seems to say that there is an important role of God's children in restoring God's creation. The creation will be renewed through the work of God's children. Eventually, on the Parousia, "the creation itself will be set free from its bondage to decay and will obtain the freedom of the glory of the children of God" (8:21). On this day, there will be also the redemption of the bodies, which must be understood from the perspective of 1 Cor 15:44 in which the resurrection body is "a spiritual body" (*soma pneumatikon*). That is, the redeemed body is not the recovery of the human body (i.e., flesh). But this body (*soma*) is a new kind of the body, not the same as the human body. The earthly body is the body known to people, which is "a physical body" (*soma psychikon*). According to Paul, children of God are hopeful in God no matter what, as 8:24–25 says: "For in hope we were saved. Now hope that is seen is not hope. For who hopes for what is seen? But if we hope for what we do not see, we wait for it with patience." It is in hope that they can live without worries about the future. The Spirit is behind all they do, helping them in their weakness. Even though they do not know how to pray, the Spirit intercedes for them according to the will of God (8:26–27).

A, 8:28–39 Assurance of the Love of God in Christ

8:28–39 constitutes a chiasmus A that strengthens the love of God in Christ. Paul stated in the beginning of Rom 8 that Christians are not condemned anymore because they are in Christ Jesus (8:1). In 8:1–4 (A), he emphasized the new life in the Spirit and in Christ. 8:28–39 strengthens this point by talking about God's providential love and care as well as about the love of Christ. In 8:28–34, the main topic is God's love for his children. The central verses are 8:33–34a: "Who will bring any charge against God's elect? It is God who justifies. Who is to condemn?" Those who come to God by grace through Christ are not condemned because God is the one who justifies. He uses the first person plural and confirms the love of God: "We know that all things work together for good for those who love God, who are called according to his purpose" (8:28). "We know" is an experiential language; it is like "we confess." More than that, the point is all things work together for good "for those who love God, who are called according to his purpose." In other words, we cannot merely say all things work together for Christians; but we have to say all things work together *for those who love God, who are called according to this purpose.* Many would say that they love God, but often they do not do the work of God according to his purpose. Therefore, they must know what God wants. This is an important condition for accomplishing all things. But the caution is we cannot assume that we can know fully all about God. Even though Paul, in 8:29–30, talks about God's foreknowledge, predestination, calling, justification and glorification for his children, it is God's business that we cannot know fully. Therefore, this section must be read confessionally and contextually. The confessional and contextual reading means that one has to look at himself or herself alone without generalizing about God's mind or plan. In other words, Paul does not seem to think about the doctrine of predestination here. His basic point is God's love is secured in Christ and the Spirit.

In 8:34b–37, Paul emphasizes Christ Jesus's intercession for Christians. He became the spirit (c.f., 1 Cor 15:45) and can help his followers. He asks a rhetorical question: "Who will separate us from the love of Christ? Will hardship, or distress, or persecution, or famine, or nakedness, or peril, or sword? . . . No, in all these things we are more than conquerors through him who loved us" (8:35–37). Under any circumstances, God's love in Christ will not change.

Then, finally, Paul comes back to the love of God in Christ: "For I am convinced that neither death, nor life, nor angels, nor rulers, nor things present, nor things to come, nor powers, nor height, nor depth, nor anything else in all creation, will be able to separate us from the love of God in Christ Jesus our Lord" (8:38–39). Paul reinforces God's love in Christ. God's love was proved through the work of Christ (c.f., 5:6–10). Therefore, he speaks up for God's children: "What then are we to say about these things? If God is for us, who is against us? He who did not withhold his own Son, but gave him up for all of us, will he not with him also give us everything else? Who will bring any charge against God's elect? It is God who justifies. Who is to condemn?" (8:31–34).

9:1–29 THE DILEMMA OF ISRAEL
IN THE GOSPEL OF GOD

After a long discussion about the gospel of God in Rom 1–8, Paul still has a few more important things to say to Roman Christians such as the place of Israel in the gospel of God (Rom 9–11); individual and communal ethics in the gospel of God (Rom 12–15); and his passion to take this gospel to Spain (Rom 15). Rom 1–8 does not conclude the gospel of God or the gospel of faith even though Rom 8 looks like the end of the letter. At a glance, many interpreters think Rom 1–8 deals with the center of Paul's gospel, which is about "justification by faith" from a forensic salvation perspective. But this view does not stand ground for two reasons. One is, as we saw in the previous chapters, Paul's concept of justification has more to do with a right relationship with God than the legal standing in the court. The other reason is that Paul's gospel of faith needs to include the salvation of Israel. He has no intention to exclude it on the basis of what he sees now. He believes that God will do something about his people. Therefore, Rom 1–11 as a whole must be seen as the heart of Paul's gospel.

But it does not mean that Paul did not deal with this issue of the salvation of Israel in Rom 1–8. From the beginning of the letter, he stated that the power of God for salvation needs to reach all, "to the Jew first and also the Greek" (1:16). He argues that Jesus proclaimed the good news of God and revealed his righteousness through faithfulness. God will justify those who have the faithfulness of Jesus. Anyone can be hopeful in this gospel of God through faith. Then, some Gentile Christians in Rome assume that Paul's gospel does not need the law because Judaism is outdated. Or, even some think God abandoned them. So, Paul raised questions to them in 3:1–3: "Then what advantage has the Jew? Or what is the value of circumcision? Much, in every way. For in the first place the Jews were entrusted with the oracles of God. What if some were unfaithful? Will their faithlessness nullify the faithfulness of God?"

As we see above, in Rom 1–8, Paul partially dealt with this issue of Israel in the gospel of God. Therefore, he needs Rom 9–11 where he will fully explore it. Paul as a Jew has concerns about his own people because they are God's covenanted people. He raised questions such as the following: Does God not care about Jews who do not follow Jesus as the Messiah? Does God nullify the Abrahamic covenant with his descendants?

Paul's dilemma is why Israelites do not turn to Jesus the Messiah even though they were descendants of Abraham. Did God's word fail? (9:5). His answer is "by no means!" because there is a difference between the children of the flesh and the children of the promise. "The children of the flesh" means those who live according to the flesh (c.f., 8:5). But the true children of God are the children of the promise, who accept God's grace and follow him. The children of God set their minds on the things of the Spirit (8:5). Likewise, as we saw in Rom 8:14, "all who are led by the Spirit of God are children of God."

Paul's point is, nevertheless, the word of God did not fail because God is sovereign and merciful. Though Paul does not suggest that all Jews and all Gentiles are automatically included in the children of God because there should be a human response, he leaves room for God to act toward the salvation of all, including Israel. He has a strong belief about the salvation of Israel and yet he also has a bitter feeling about the current status of his fellow Jews. For example, he says in 11:1–2: "I ask, then, has God rejected his people? By no means! I myself am an Israelite, a descendant of Abraham, a member of the tribe of Benjamin. God has not rejected his people whom he foreknew. Do you not know what the scripture says of Elijah, how he pleads with God against Israel?"

Outline of Rom 9:1–29

9:1–5   The dilemma of Israel in the gospel of God
9:6–13   The word of God did not fail
9:14–24   God's sovereign mercy and providence
9:25–29   The result of God's sovereignty and providence
   9:25–26   Gentiles called as children of the living God
   9:27–28   Salvation of a remnant of Israel

9:1–5 The dilemma of Israel in the Gospel of God

9:1–5 sets the tone for Rom 9–11 because here Paul talks about his great sorrow and deep anguish due to his own people (Israelites) many of whom are not yet in Christ. This is a dilemma for him because, on the one hand, they are people of God: "They are Israelites, and to them belong the adoption, the glory, the covenants, the giving of the law, the worship, and the promises; to them belong the patriarchs, and from them, according to the flesh, comes the Messiah" (9:4–5). But on the other hand, they do not confess that Jesus is the Messiah in the present. This dilemma causes him to use very emotional language to appeal to his audience in Rome: "I am speaking the truth in Christ—I am not lying; my conscience confirms it by the Holy Spirit— I have great sorrow and unceasing anguish in my heart" (9:1–2). It is interesting that he uses "the truth in Christ" in Rom 9:1 to emphasize his personal feeling of sorrow and anguish due to his own people. Usually, he uses the phrase "in Christ" to emphasize Christian life needing Christ-like life (for example, 8:1). Furthermore, he says, "I am not lying; my conscience confirms it by the Holy Spirit." This is because some people will not believe what he says about his own people. All his point is he is serious about his own people, Israelites. Then, he puts himself in the position of Moses who sought to save Israelites from God's punishment by offering his name cut off from the book of life (Exod 32:32), saying: "For I could wish that I myself were accursed and cut off from Christ for the sake of my own people, my kindred according to the flesh" (9:3). In fact, he distinguishes between the children of the flesh and the children of the promise. That is, not all Israelites are automatically the children of God. Paul's statement is unlike Moses's because he considers Israelites as "my kindred according to the flesh." While Moses risked his name cut off from the book, Paul wishes him to be "cut off from Christ for the sake of my own people." The difference is Paul's wish is based on a Christ-centered mission.[75] Nevertheless, what both Moses and Paul have in common is their self-sacrifice attitude toward Jews in general.

9:6–13 The Word of God Did Not Fail

Stating that the word of God did not fail, Paul responds to two different groups of the people: those who misunderstand Paul's gospel (mainly, Gentile Christians) and those who reject his gospel (mainly, Jewish Christians). The former group thinks that Paul's gospel is by faith alone through Christ and that God abandoned Jews who do not have faith. They think God nullified his covenant with Abraham and his descendants. But this is not the case, as Paul says in 11:1–2: "I ask, then, has God rejected his people? By no means! I myself am an Israelite, a descendant of Abraham, a member of the tribe of Benjamin. God has not rejected his people whom he foreknew. Do you not know what the scripture says of Elijah, how he pleads with God against Israel?" (c.f., 3:1–3). Even though many Israelites do not come to Christ right now, it is possible that they still may be saved with God's providential care (c.f., 11:26). Therefore, Gentile Christians cannot say that the word of God failed on the basis of what they see now. Paul maintains hope about his own people because God is sovereign, merciful, and free. We will see more about this issue in Rom 11.

Those who reject Paul's gospel are primarily Jewish Christians and his fellow Jews who think that he rejects the law and does not fully appreciate God's covenant with Abraham and his descendants. They believe that all Israelites are the children of God—the children of the promise of God through Abraham. But they hear those who follow Jesus through faith are the children of God. Similarly, they hear those who live according to the Spirit are children of God (8:5–14). If this were the case, they thought, the word of God failed to them. Gentile Christians also thought that the word of God failed for a different reason that Jews had no faith. But Paul responds to Jews and Gentiles that the word of God did not fail. He argues

---

75. As Gal 2:20 implies, it is impossible to live without Christ: "and it is no longer I who live, but it is Christ who lives in me. And the life I now live in the flesh I live by the faith of the Son of God, who loved me and gave himself for me."

that there is a difference between the true descendants of Abraham who comes through the promise of God and the children of the flesh who stay outside of the promise of God (9:6a; Gen 21:12). So Isaac is a child born through the promise of God (9:9; Gen 18:10–14), and thus his descendants through the same promise of God will continue to be children of God. The implication here is that Ishmael is not a child of the promise. Accordingly, Jacob is the blessing line whereas Esau is not included in that line (9:10–13; Gen 25:23; Mal 1:2–3). Paul's point is the true children of God come through the promise of God, not by human action or any other thing (9:9–13).

Obviously, his argument about the true children of God seems not very persuasive to Jews or others because the promise of God can be the language of arbitrariness. The question is, for example, why was Jacob chosen while Esau was not? Is it fair? In some sense, a theology, including Paul's, is a response to the reality in the past where some were obedient to God while others were not. Those who were obedient are considered the children of the promise. But Paul goes one step further and argues that the promise of God must be the basis of faith. In other words, the basis of faith is not the law or rituals or any other thing than faith, which is to trust God and his promise. Through this logic, Paul extends God's promise to Gentiles.

9:14–24 God's Sovereign Mercy and Providence

In 9:14, Paul asks rhetorical questions about God: "What then are we to say? Is there injustice on God's part?" The answer is "by no means!" He explains in 9:14–18 that God is not unjust because his purpose is to save people through his mercy. For example, God's sovereignty or freedom is used for delivering his people from bondage to Egypt. God says to Moses: "I will have mercy on whom I have mercy, and I will have compassion on whom I have compassion" (9:15; Exod 33:19). It is God's sole decision that he will have mercy and compassion on a particular people. Pharaoh could not prevent them from leaving his country because the sovereign God acts toward his people. In the process of the deliverance of his people, God's power was manifested because of Pharaoh's hardening (Exod 9:16). Paul's point is not that God can do anything he wishes but that he works toward saving his people through his mercy. In other words, God's sovereignty and mercy are used for saving his people.[76] As a result, God's power of salvation is manifested in the world and his name is proclaimed in all the earth (9:17). Equally important, his point is not that God loves only Israelites or particular people but that God wants both Jews and Gentiles to be saved.

Then, in 9:19, Paul raises rhetorical questions about God's fairness and human responsibility: "Why then does he still find fault? For who can resist his will?" In other words, if God plans everything beforehand and does it himself, why is there still human responsibility for wrongdoing? Regarding this issue, Paul defends God's absolute freedom and sovereignty by alluding to the story of the potter and clay in Isaiah 29:16: "But who indeed are you, a human being, to argue with God? Will what is molded say to the one who molds it, 'Why have you made me like this?' Has the potter no right over the clay, to make out of the same lump one object for special use and another for ordinary use?" (9:20–21). It seems that God can do anything with his freedom. But this is not the point because Paul argues, as he did in 9:14–18, that God's sovereignty has a purpose of calling and saving people. This point is further argued in 9:22–24. In this text, Paul believes that God has endured the objects of wrath with much patience to reveal his power and that "he has done so in order to make known the riches of his glory for the objects of mercy" (9:23). In other words, God's purpose is not merely to punish people but to save them; as a result, his power and glory are powerfully manifested in the world. This grace of God enables Gentiles also to receive his calling and mercy (9:24).

9:25–29 The Result of God's Sovereignty and Providence

9:25–26 Gentiles Called as Children of the Living God

Paul now argues that Gentiles can be also called children of the living God because of God's sovereignty and mercy (9:26). This is not a strange idea from his perspective, as he already stated in 3:29–30: "Or is God the God of Jews only? Is he not the God of Gentiles also? Yes, of Gentiles also, since God is one; and he will justify the circumcised on the ground of faith and the uncircumcised through that same faith." To support his position about Gentile inclusion to the people of God, Paul quotes Hosea and says in 9:25–26: "Those who were not my people I will call 'my people,' and her who was not beloved I will call 'beloved.' And in the very place where it was

---

76. Jewett, *Romans*, 573.

said to them, 'You are not my people,' there they shall be called children of the living God."

9:27–28: Salvation of a Remnant of Israel

In 9:6–18, Paul argued that even if Israelites are descendants of Abraham, they are not all the children of God because the true children of God are the children of the promise, which is different from the children of the flesh. In 9:27–28, Paul gives another reason that not all Israelites are children of God by quoting Isaiah 10:22: "And Isaiah cries out concerning Israel, 'Though the number of the children of Israel were like the sand of the sea, only a remnant of them will be saved; for the Lord will execute his sentence on the earth quickly and decisively.'" This statement reflects the history of Israel in which there have been blessings and punishments depending on their behavior. Paul, standing in first century CE, reflects on the past history of Israel and finds it true that not all Israelites were saved. Many of them were destroyed in wars due to their evil and disobedience to God. Some were taken into Babylon as an exile after the fall of Jerusalem. There will be God's judgment on all evil: "for the Lord will execute his sentence on the earth quickly and decisively." All this implies that there will be a consequence of human behavior. But as time goes by, people have to see new hope in God. Now a theology of hope and a remnant salvation emerges. A remnant theology implicates the human responsibility for God's grace. Eventually, Paul's point is both God's grace and human response are important. So, again, Paul quotes from Isaiah: "And as Isaiah predicted, 'If the Lord of hosts had not left survivors to us, we would have fared like Sodom and been made like Gomorrah.'"

9:30–10:21 RIGHTEOUSNESS FOR JEW AND GENTILE THROUGH FAITH

In 9:27–28, Paul talked about a remnant salvation, based on God's grace. But even in this grace of God, the painful reality is not all of Israelites were saved. This is because not all of them were faithful to God. In 9:30–33, Paul explains why Jews failed to attain righteousness even though they strove for it. It is because they strove for it on the basis of the law or works, not on the basis of faith. On the other hand, Gentiles could attain righteousness through faith, which means trusting God and following Jesus. But in

10:1–3, Paul expresses his heart's desire and prayer to God so that his own people, Jews, may be saved. Then, in 10:4–13, he explains again that faith through Christ is the answer to the human predicament. Christ fulfills the law and anyone who follows him will live a life of righteousness that comes from God. And "there is no distinction between Jew and Greek" (10:12). Finally, in 10:14–21, he comes again to the reality that not all Jews accept Jesus as the Messiah. Even though there was good news available to them, not all have obeyed it (10:15–18). Then, he introduces a motif of Jews' jealousy toward Gentiles because of their salvation (10:19–20). This motif is fully explored in Rom 11.

Outline of 9:30—10:21

9:30–33   Why Israel failed about righteousness
10:1–3   Paul's wish for the salvation of Israel and their predicament
10:4–13   Righteousness for all, Jew and Gentile, from faith through Christ
10:14–21   But not all have obeyed the good news

Rom 9:30–33 Why Israel Failed about Righteousness

Paul begins with rhetorical questions in 9:30–31: "What then are we to say? Gentiles, who did not strive for righteousness, have attained it, that is, righteousness through faith; but Israel, who did strive for the righteousness that is based on the law, did not succeed in fulfilling that law. Why not?" Earlier, in 9:14–29, he told his audience that God has freedom and mercy toward humanity. The claim that Gentiles are also called the children of God troubles many Jews because only Jews are the descendants of Abraham. But in Paul's view, true children of God are not the children of the flesh. The problem is they strive for righteousness. For example, if they elevate particular laws at the expense of God's impartial love for all, that is unacceptable to God. The law must be a protector of faith so that God's love and justice are extended to all. The law follows faith (c.f., Rom 4). In other words, the law must be kept through the lens of faith that God is loved and neighbors are respected. So, Paul states Jews did not succeed in fulfilling that law "because they did not strive for it on the basis of faith, but as if it were based on works" (9:31–32). In contrast, Gentiles "did not strive for righteousness," but have attained it through faith (Rom 9:30).

Through faith, God's righteousness can be part of human life. While the law is needed to human life, it does not precede faith focused on God. But Jews changed this order between faith and the law; their priority was the law, resulting in stumbling over the stone. Paul quotes from Isa 8:14: "See, I am laying in Zion a stone that will make people stumble, a rock that will make them fall, and whoever believes in him will not be put to shame" (9:33). On the one hand, it is God's action that makes them fall. This seems to support Paul's earlier view of God's sovereignty. But in fact, their stumbling over the stone happened because they did not believe in God, as Isaiah says in 9:33: "and whoever believes in him will not be put to shame."

10:1–3 Paul's Wish for Salvation of Israel and Their Predicament

In 10:1, Paul once again, as he did in 9:1–2, expresses his emotions about his own people, saying "my heart's desire and prayer to God for them is that they may be saved." But he realizes that they have a zeal for God, which is not enlightened (10:2). That is, their problem is to establish their own righteousness.[77] According to Paul, they are "ignorant of the righteousness that comes from God" and that "they have not submitted to God's righteousness" (10:3). The problem is their absolutizing of the law without submitting to God's righteousness (10:3). In 10:3, Paul distinguishes between "the righteousness that comes from God" and "their own righteousness" (10:3). The former means that God is the one who is righteous and that one must live by faith to be part of God's righteousness. God is sovereign, merciful, and free. No one speaks for him. The only thing needed by humanity is to accept his rule. In other words, people have to have faith in him. Then, they may be justified by God. In sum, "the righteousness that comes from God" means all things should be done through faith in God, which means trusting God and submitting to his righteousness. In contrast, seeking "their own righteousness" means "they are the center of the righteousness." So, they must be open to God's greater purpose of saving all peoples and seek the God-centered righteousness.

---

77. E. P. Sanders, "Covenantal Nomism Revisited," 23–55.

10:4–13 Righteousness for All, Jew and Gentile, from Faith through Christ

Having explained why Jews did not attain the righteousness and why they did not succeed in fulfilling the law, Paul elucidates, in 10:4–13, the importance of faith for all, Jew and Gentile, through Christ. He says in 10:4: "For Christ is the fulfillment (*telos*) of the law so that there may be righteousness for everyone who believes." This verse must be understood with 8:1–3, which shows God's dealing with and condemning of sin in the flesh because of Jesus's work that made possible freedom from the law of sin and of death" (8:2). Then, in 8:3, Paul says: "For God has done what the law, weakened by the flesh, could not do: by sending his own Son in the likeness of sinful flesh, and to deal with sin, he condemned sin in the flesh." Jesus defeated sin and submitted to God's righteousness. As a result, "the just requirement of the law is fulfilled in those who "walk not according to the flesh but according to the Spirit" (8:4). The requirement of the law has to do with the love of God and the love of neighbor (c.f., 13:8–10). As Christ fulfilled the law through faith, his followers also have to do the same thing.

Likewise, Paul makes a distinction between "the righteousness that comes from the law" and "the righteousness that comes from faith" (10:5–6). The former means the self-centered, law-centered, and works-centered righteousness, as Paul explored them in 3:27–31. In contrast, the latter means the God-centered, faith-driven righteousness. In other words, the law should be fulfilled through faith and love (c.f., 10:4). However, "the righteousness that comes from faith" should not be understood as the doctrine of "justification by faith," as we saw in 1:17 and 3:21–22. For Paul, faith means to trust God and follow Jesus Christ.

Then, Paul emphasizes faith with a focus on its content and benefit. First, in 10:8b, he uses *rema* ("the word") to explain faith. He says *rema* is "the word of faith" that is proclaimed by the followers of Jesus. *Rema* is different from the law or works of the law because faith informs "the word." In other words, all sayings and deeds must be done through the lens of faith, which orients a person's mind and heart toward God. Also, this lens of faith must see what Christ has done for God's righteousness. Christians proclaim what God has done through his Son Jesus.

Second, Paul says this word is "near you, on your lips and in your heart" (10:8). This means that "the word of faith" must be part of everyday life. "Near you" means Christians must live with it in their workplace. "On your lips" means that the truth of the gospel must be spoken boldly in public space, in streets or in shops. But this proclamation of the word comes out of the heart (*kardia*) because the word is "in your heart" (10:8). This implies that every spoken word of faith must reflect the deep inside of the heart where the Spirit dwells.

Third, in 10:9, Paul explains what it means to have faith: "because if you confess with your lips that Jesus is Lord and believe in your heart that God raised him from the dead, you will be saved." Faith involves specific content and action. A person must confess that Jesus is Lord (*kyrios*). This means the real Lord is not the emperor or any human master but Jesus Christ who exemplified God's love and his righteousness. Because of this confession, a person must live by the spirit of Jesus. Likewise, a person must believe in his/her heart that "God raised him [Jesus] from the dead." Here faith means to acknowledge the power of God and to trust him. God raised Jesus from the dead and exalted him. Jesus did not fail on the cross; he revealed God's righteousness. In sum, faith means to trust God and to live with the lordship of Christ. Christians must be ruled by Jesus or his spirit, not by their sinful passions (6:6; 7:5). Then, they "will be saved" (10:9). Salvation is not a once-and-for-all event. Justification and salvation have to be worked out in everyday life until the Parousia. 10:10 emphasizes this point: "For one believes with the heart and so is justified, and one confesses with the mouth and so is saved." Notice here that justification and salvation are made with the present tenses ("so is justified" and "so is saved").

Fourth, in 10:11–13, Paul states the power of the gospel of faith. In 10:11, he quotes from Isa 28:16: "No one who believes in him will be put to shame." This verse also echoes 8:1: "There is therefore now no condemnation for those who are in Christ Jesus." "Believing in him" in 10:11 means recognizing the works of Jesus for God's righteousness and following his spirit. Those who are in Christ are not condemned because they live in the Spirit. In 10:12, Paul says: "For there is no distinction between Jew and Greek; the same Lord is Lord of all and is generous to all who call on him." This verse refers to what he said earlier in 1:16 and 3:29–30 where he emphasized the gospel of faith for all. In 10:13, he quotes from Joel 2:32: "Everyone who calls on the name of the Lord shall be saved." This verse means that the gospel of faith is open to all, but there must be a proper response, which is to call on the name of the Lord. Obviously, "to call on the name of the Lord" means understanding Jesus's work, following his spirit, and living under the lordship of Christ.

10:14–21 But Not All Have Obeyed the Good News

Paul realizes that not all Jews accepted the good news coming through Christ's word. But in fact, the good news has been proclaimed long before Jesus, as Paul quotes from Isaiah: "How beautiful upon the mountains are the feet of the messenger who announces peace, who brings good news, who announces salvation, who says to Zion, 'Your God reigns.'" (Isa 52:7). Isaiah says the good news comes from God, and it is about the salvation of Israel and God's reign. Paul also quotes from Joel 2:32: "Then everyone who calls on the name of the Lord shall be saved; for in Mount Zion and in Jerusalem there shall be those who escape, as the Lord has said, and among the survivors shall be those whom the Lord calls." In Joel, the emphasis is the faith that calls on the name of the Lord. This implies that not all can be saved. Quoting these prophetic words, Paul emphasizes that the good news has been available and proclaimed through prophets long before Jesus and that faith is required to realize that good news.

But the irony is, as Paul states in 10:16: "not all have obeyed the good news," quoting from Isa 53:1: "Who has believed what we have heard?" He knows that not all Jews accepted the good news of God through Christ. But we should notice the verb "to obey" (*hypakouo*) in 10:16, which seems to be intentional by Paul because "the obedience of faith" (*hypakoen pisteos*) was used earlier in 1:5.[78] That is, what is required is the obedience of faith that people submit to God's righteousness. In 10:3, Paul pointed out the problem of Jews who sought to establish their own righteousness, not based on faith. Similarly, in 6:15–23, we also saw about faith's obedience to God's righteousness. Faith is not the information about God or Christ but a commitment to seek God's righteousness. We also saw the importance of submitting to God's law in 8:7: "For this reason the mind that is set on the flesh is hostile to God; it does not submit to God's law—indeed it cannot."

Then, in 10:17, Paul relates the obedience of faith to "the word of Christ": "Faith comes from what is heard, and what is heard comes through the word of God." Now "the word of Christ" is a genitive phrase, which can be either a subjective genitive (Christ's word) or an objective genitive (the word about Christ).[79] While the latter is not impossible, the former must be best understood. That is, "Christ's word" (a subjective genitive) reminds us of his initial proclamation of "the good news of God" (c.f., Mark

78. Keck, *Romans*, 259.
79. Ibid., 260.

1:14–15). Jesus declared God's time and his rule has come and asked his audience to change their mind toward God. If we understand Christ's word as his preaching about the rule of God in the here and now, what he said and did constitutes his faithfulness.

Paul often uses the phrase "the gospel of Christ" in his letters, which can be also understood as similar to Christ's word, because "the gospel of Christ" can be a subjective genitive: the good news of God that Christ proclaimed. In fact, 1:1 begins with the good news of God for which Paul was set apart, and this good news concerns his Son (1:3). A few verses later, Paul also talks about "the gospel of his Son" (1:9), which must be the good news that his Son carried out: "For God, whom I serve with my spirit by announcing *the gospel of his Son*, is my witness that without ceasing I remember you always in my prayers."

"The gospel of his Son" is what Jesus brought God's good news to the world; in other words, it is not about him but about his work of God. First Corinthians 9:12 reads: "If others share this rightful claim on you, do not we still more? Nevertheless, we have not made use of this right, but we endure anything rather than put an obstacle in the way of the gospel of Christ." Second Corinthians 9:13 also reads: "Through the testing of this ministry you glorify God by your obedience to the confession of the gospel of Christ and by the generosity of your sharing with them and with all others." Here, Paul's point is that the Corinthians must return to the faith and spirit of Christ because they moved away from Christ's faith. Galatians 1:7 also reads: "not that there is another gospel, but there are some who are confusing you and want to pervert the gospel of Christ." Some Galatians (Jewish Christians or Christian Jews) taught that Gentiles also need circumcision to belong to Christ. But Paul says that is a perversion of the good news that Jesus taught, as Gal 2:16 implies: "Yet we know that a person is justified not by the works of the law but through *the faith of Jesus Christ*. And we have come to believe in Christ Jesus, so that we might be justified by *the faith of Christ*, and not by doing the works of the law, because no one will be justified by the works of the law" (Italics are my translation and for emphasis; these translations are of a subjective genitive understanding; that is, Paul talks about Christ's faith).

Philippians 1:27 also reads: "Only, live your life in a manner worthy of the gospel of Christ, so that, whether I come and see you or am absent and hear about you, I will know that you are standing firm in one spirit, striving side by side with one mind for the faith of the gospel." Here also,

Paul talks about the manner of life that is based on what Christ taught and preached: Christ's good news. Lastly, First Thessalonians 3:2 reads: "and we sent Timothy, our brother and co-worker for God in proclaiming the gospel of Christ, to strengthen and encourage you for the sake of your faith." Here also, a better understanding of "the gospel of Christ" is Christ's good news, namely what he did for God as his Son.

In 10:18–21, Paul asks about his own people: "Have they not heard?" (10:18); "Did Israel not understand?" (10:19). The answer is that they have heard and understood the good news. The good news of God through Jesus Christ has been proclaimed throughout the major cities in the Roman Empire. It is Paul's exaggeration that the good news reached all the earth (10:18). But his point is it has been widely available throughout the regions. But Jews did not accept the good news of God in their lives. They served idols and did not honor God (Deut 32:21). They are "a perverse generation, children in whom there is no faithfulness" (Deut 32:20). So what is needed to God's people is obedience and faithfulness to God. Otherwise, God can be found to the one who asks for and calls on his name, as Paul quotes from Isa 65:1–2: "I was ready to be sought out by those who did not ask, to be found by those who did not seek me. I said, 'Here I am, here I am,' to a nation that did not call on my name. I held out my hands all day long to a rebellious people, who walk in a way that is not good, following their own devices."

Here, Paul thinks of the two different realities in the present, as he already stated in 9:30–33. That is, whereas Gentiles attained the righteousness through faith even though they did not strive for it, Jews strove for the righteousness on the basis of the law but failed to attain it. Again, this is the dilemma for Paul that refers back to 9:1–29. For the time being, God has held out his hands "to a disobedient and contrary people" (10:21). Then, how long will God of Jews hold out his hands to his disobedient people? For some time only or forever? These questions will be answered in Romans 11.

11:1–36 THE MYSTERY OF SALVATION OF ISRAEL

"The gospel of God" that Paul started exploring in Rom 1:1 and throughout Rom 1–10 reaches its climax in chapter 11 because God's gospel needs the salvation of Israel. Paul begins with the question "Has God rejected his people?" (11:1). The answer is "by no means!" Then he warns Gentile Christians that God is still faithful to them, reminding them God wants the salvation of both Jews and Gentiles. Then he ends with a doxology in 11:33–36 that says God's wisdom and knowledge are unfathomably deep. No one takes the place of God. God's way is beyond humans and the human job is to trust God and participate in Christ's faithfulness. No one can boast about his/her salvation, based on his/her background. God is the source of salvation and it is for everyone who has faith.

Paul believes that his successful ministry for Gentiles will make his own people jealous so that some of them might be saved (11:14). In other words, he thinks all things can and must work together for the salvation of many. He thinks in terms of God's providence in that Jews' trespass or tumbling opened a road to Gentile salvation, which then makes Jews jealous. He even believes that God will save all Israel (11:26). This belief represents Paul's hope and prayer that all Israelites will be saved. Gentiles are grafted to branches of an olive tree while some natural branches were cut off for a while. But eventually, those cut-off branches will be grafted back onto it by God's mysterious involvement. Then, the gospel completes its cycle. Until then, he has a job to do: his diligent work for Gentiles and his plan to go to Spain to proclaim God's good news through Jesus Christ.

Outline of 11:1–36

11:1–10   God has not rejected his people
11:11–24   The purpose of Jews' stumbling
11:25–32   The mystery of God's salvation of Israel
11:33–36   Doxology: God's wisdom, his knowledge, his judgments, and his way

11:1–10 God Has Not Rejected His People

In 11:1, Paul begins with a question: "I ask, has God rejected his people?" This question is a response to 10:20–21 in which he said that Gentiles found God and that God has held out his hands to "a disobedient and contrary people." The above question also refers to 9:30–33 in which he said that Israelites strove for the righteousness but they did not attain it because they sought on the basis of the law. From the above reference texts, Paul's rhetorical question is twofold: 1) Has God rejected his people as a whole and forever?; 2) Will he not save them all in the future? His answer is "By no means! I myself am an Israelite, a descendant of Abraham, a member of the tribe of Benjamin" (11:1). His emphasis on his Jewish ethnicity with a sense of Abrahamic lineage sounds a bit awkward because, earlier in 9:6–8, he told his readers that "For not all Israelites truly belong to Israel, and not all of Abraham's children are his true descendants . . . it is not the children of the flesh who are the children of God, but the children of the promise are counted as descendants." He knows from the reality that not all Israelites were saved in Jewish history and during his time. But he hopes that all may be saved (c.f., 9:3).

In 11:2–10, Paul explains why God has not rejected his people as a whole. In 11:2, he states that God foreknew them. This implies that God called and loved his people without conditions, as the Abrahamic covenant shows. Paul quotes from various scriptures and emphasizes God's unconditional love and care for his people. For example, 1 Sam 12:22 reads: "For the Lord will not cast away his people, for his great name's sake, because it has pleased the Lord to make you a people for himself. Ps 94:14 strikes a similar chord: "For the Lord will not forsake his people; he will not abandon his heritage." Even if not all Israelites may be saved, God is still on his decision to save them all in the future. This reality creates a theology of remnant, as Paul already did in 9:27–28. Here in 11:2b-4 again, he talks about that same theology, referring to Elijah's episode in 1 Kings 19:10:

> 2 Do you not know what the scripture says of Elijah, how he pleads with God against Israel? 3 "Lord, they have killed your prophets, they have demolished your altars; I alone am left, and they are seeking my life." 4 But what is the divine reply to him? "I have kept for myself seven thousand who have not bowed the knee to Baal."

Elijah feels all ended with failure because Jezebel tried to kill him. Moreover, he says that Israelites killed God's prophets and demolished his altars. Elijah is left alone. But God says to him that he saved a remnant of seven thousand who will continue Israel by God's grace. In 11:5, Paul applies this story to the current situation during his time; namely, he believes that there is also a remnant at the present. This means not all Jews are saved. Then the questions are: Whose fault is this? "What then? Israel failed to obtain what it was seeking" (11:7). In other words, if Israel is God's chosen, why does God not save all? Paul's answer has a double entendre. On the one hand, he seems to say everything is done by God, as he quotes: "God gave them a sluggish spirit, eyes that would not see and ears that would not hear, down this very day" (Deut 29:4, quoted in 11:7b–8). He also quotes from Psalm 68:22–23: "Let their table become a snare and a trap, a stumbling block and a retribution for them; let their eyes be darkened so that they cannot see, and keep their backs forever bent." On the other hand, he does not mean that Jews are not responsible for their actions. In 9:32–33, he hinted that a person is responsible for his/her life: "and whoever believes in him [God] will not be put to shame" (9:33). While God is behind every human action, it does not mean that humans are free from their fault.

11:11–24 The Purpose of Jews' Stumbling

If some were elected and others were hardened in Jewish history as we saw above, is the stumbling of some Jews final and is there no hope of salvation for them in the future? So Paul asks: "Have they stumbled so as to fall?" The answer is: "By no means! But through their stumbling salvation has come to the Gentiles, so as to make Israel jealous" (11:11). Their stumbling leads to the salvation of Gentiles. Then the success of the Gentile mission makes them jealous, so that they may also come to be saved. He is very optimistic about the fate of Israel as a whole and considers Jews' stumbling to be purposeful from God's perspective.

In 11:12–14, he argues for the necessity of salvation for both Jews and Gentiles. Even if Jews failed to fulfill the law because they strove for righteousness on the basis of works, their stumbling does not mean that they failed forever. Even their stumbling has a purpose that Gentiles are saved and that eventually, they may be as well. Because of their stumbling, the gospel spread to the Gentiles, which are "riches for the world" (11:12). But more riches are possible when Jews are included in this. Therefore, Paul asks Gentiles not to think their salvation is enough (11:13–14). He addresses them: "Now I am speaking to you Gentiles" (11:13) and tells them that his ministry for the Gentiles is not the final goal of his mission since the gospel needs Israel too. Therefore, in 11:15–16, he continues to emphasize the importance of the whole batch of the dough or the reconciliation of the world (not a partial reconciliation with a particular people). For this goal, all must work together for the wholeness of the world.

Paul also reminds Gentiles of their place in the salvation of God. In 11:17–24, he talks about the olive tree allegory and appeals to both Jews and Gentiles that they all must embrace the whole tree, including branches and the root. Israel is a natural olive tree. But in reality, not all Israelites truly belong to Israel because of their choice of evil (c.f., 9:6–13). Thus he says that "some of the branches were broken off," while other wild branches were "grafted in their place to share the rich root of the olive tree" (11:17). But Gentiles should not boast over the branches (Jews) (11:18). He goes on to say: "If you do boast, remember that it is not you that support the root, but the root that supports you" (11:18). Here, "the root" may be God's covenant with Israel and his unconditional love of them. If Gentiles ignore this, they dishonor God.

In 11:19, Paul explains why natural branches were broken off. On the one hand, they were broken off so that Gentiles might be grafted in. This idea is what he already explored in 11:11–14. That is, Jews' rejection of the gospel helps Gentiles to be saved. On the other hand, they were broken off because of their unfaithfulness. This is Paul's realism that humans are responsible for their fate. To the Gentiles, he warns that they should not become proud, but "stand in awe" (11:20). The reason is that God is fair to both Jews and Gentiles in terms of his kindness and severity (11:21–22). In other words, even the grafted branches will be cut off if they do not continue in God's kindness because he is severe toward those who have fallen. He also talks about Israel, saying that if they do not persist in unfaithfulness, they will be grafted in because God has the power to do so again. In the end, he emphasizes the importance of the whole olive tree to which both wild and natural branches were grafted, as he says in 11:24: "For if you have been cut from what is by nature a wild olive tree and grafted, contrary to nature, into a cultivated olive tree, how much more will these natural branches be grafted back into their own olive tree." Paul's warning is that the present reality does not decide their fate forever.

11:25–32 The Mystery of God's Salvation of Israel

In 11:25–32, Paul talks about the future state of Israel and hopes that "all Israel" will be saved (11:26). "All Israel" may be close to a collective term "my people" (Exod 3:7, 10; 6:7; Lev 26:12; 2 Chr 6:5–6). He thinks of God's sovereignty and mercy that makes their salvation possible. He knows it is not easy, but he hopes for the salvation of all. So it is a mystery that God will do something about his people. Therefore, in 11:25, he says to Gentile Christians: "So that you may not claim to be wiser than you are, brothers and sisters, I want you to understand this mystery: a hardening has come upon part of Israel until the full number of the Gentiles has come in." We do not know what "the full number of the Gentiles" means by Paul. Probably, he means that there are the elect from God's point. But from a human perspective, we should not pretend to know that number. But his point is that a hardening is temporary and eventually, "all Israel will be saved." He does not add "through faith" to their salvation. But this does not mean that he thinks of other means of salvation to them. In fact, here his focus is not on how they may be saved but when their salvation happens. Otherwise, throughout Romans, he was consistent arguing that both Jews and Gentiles need faithfulness to be justified by God (c.f., 3:21–26; 10:1–13). His eyes is fixed on the future state of Israel, as he quotes from Isa 59:20–21: "Out of Zion will come the Deliverer; he will banish ungodliness from Jacob"; "And this is my covenant with them, when I take away their sins" (c.f., Jer 31:31–34).

In 11:28–32, he repeats the cooperative nature of the gospel of God between Jew and Gentile. That is, Jews' rejection helps Gentiles to be the children of God. But their rejection should not be considered a permanent separation from God (11:28). Their "gifts and calling of God are irrevocable" (11:29). God's covenant remains effective to his people. In God's providence, all must work together so that both Jews and Gentiles may be saved. This point is stated in 11:30–32: "Just as you were once disobedient to God but now have received mercy because of their disobedience, so they have now been disobedient in order that, by the mercy shown to you, they too may now receive mercy. For God has imprisoned all in disobedience so that he may be merciful to all."

11:33–36 Doxology: God's Wisdom, Judgments, and Ways

After a long discussion about the place of Israel in the gospel of God, Paul ends with the doxology in 11:33–36 and drives home the importance of God's wisdom, judgments, and way, quoting from Isa 40:13 and Job 41:3:

> 33 O the depth of the riches and wisdom and knowledge of God! How unsearchable are his judgments and how inscrutable his ways! 34 "For who has known the mind of the Lord? Or who has been his counselor?" 35 "Or who has given a gift to him, to receive a gift in return?" 36 For from him and through him and to him are all things. To him be the glory forever. Amen.

God's own wisdom, judgments, and ways go beyond human thinking and judgments. Therefore, no one can take the place of God or pretend to know all about God's mind. God's salvation for all is a mystery that both Jews and Gentiles have to embrace in awe and live humbly before God. Thus his final word "Amen" closes all his previous talks and arguments. In other words, his principal argument about the gospel he began in 1:1 and throughout Romans ends here with Rom 11:36. Rom 12–16 deals with concluding matters including the gospel's power of transformation and Paul's passion to share the gospel in Spain.

SECTION III

12:1–15:13
The Gospel's Power of Transformation

AFTER A LONG DISCUSSION about the gospel of God (Rom 1–11), Paul moves on to another topic in 12:1–15:13, that is, the gospel's power of transformation in community and society. Thus he begins in 12:1–2: "I appeal to you therefore, brothers and sisters, by the mercies of God, to present your bodies as a living sacrifice, holy and acceptable to God, which is your reasonable worship. Do not be conformed to this world, but be transformed by the renewing of your minds, so that you may discern what is the will of God—what is good and acceptable and perfect." "Appealing to you therefore" is an exhortation that is based on all his previous gospel discussion in Rom 1–11. The essence of his gospel may be summarized as follows. God's good news was proclaimed by Jesus, who disclosed his righteousness through faithfulness. God justifies the one who shares the faithfulness of Jesus (3:26). Therefore, Paul is not ashamed of the gospel because it is "the power of God for salvation to everyone who has faith, to the Jew first and also to the Greek" (1:16). There is no distinction between Jews and Gentiles or between Greeks and barbarians because all can be hopeful in God through faithfulness. The common human problem is unfaithfulness/disobedience to God. While the law is holy, what must precede it is faith. While Gentiles did not receive the law, they are still held accountable for their unfaithfulness because God was revealed in nature and in their conscience. But now all can follow Christ Jesus who has revealed God's righteousness through faithfulness. As Christ died to sin and lives to God, his followers ("Christians") had died with him and live to God. "Dying to sin" means not to submit to it. They have to put death the deeds of the body by the Spirit. Then they are children of God. But this faithfulness cannot overthrow the law, and God did not reject Israel. Ultimately, God will work out the salvation of Israel. The end (*parousia*) is yet to come. Until then, both Jews and Gentiles must continue to live by faith and work together so that the mystery of God's salvation drama may unfold well.

With the above understanding of the gospel of God, which is Paul's gospel, he exhorts Roman Christians to do their best in living faithfully, presenting their bodies "as a living sacrifice, holy and acceptable to God" (12:1). He goes on to tell them not to be conformed to this world but to be transformed by the renewing of their minds (12:2). 12:1–2 sets the tone for a discussion about the gospel's power of transformation as in 12:1–15:13. Romans Christians need a new set of transformative ethics based on the gospel of God (12:3–12). For example, they must be humble toward one another (12:3); their love must be genuine (12:9); they must "live in harmony with one another" and "associate with the lowly" without claiming to be wiser than they are (12:16). Also, retaliation is prohibited (12:19), and they should "overcome evil with good" (12:21).

These transformative ethical mandates also apply to the community's dealing with the governing authorities (13:1–7). That is, they should maintain their transformative lifestyle and show the power of the gospel to the governing authorities. Otherwise, Paul's words in 13:1–7 should not be taken as a submission to abusive power. Then, he concludes his transformative ethical rules in 13:8–10: "Owe no one anything, except to love one another; for the one who loves another has fulfilled the law. The commandments, 'You shall not commit adultery; You shall not murder; You shall not steal; You shall not covet'; and any other commandment, are summed up in this word, 'Love your neighbor as yourself.' Love does no wrong to a neighbor; therefore, love is the fulfilling of the law." Paul emphasizes the love of neighbor, which sums up the whole commandments (c.f., Gal 5:14).

Outline of 12:1–15:13

12:1–2   Introduction to transformation
12:3–21   Mandates for transformative ethics
13:1–7   Dealing with the governing authorities
13:8–10   Love as the fulfilling of the law
13:11–14   Preparation for the last day

14:1–23   Welcoming those who are weak in faith

15:1–13   Following the way of Christ

12:1-2 INTRODUCTION TO TRANSFORMATION

In 12:1–2, Paul talks about specific ways that Roman Christians should honor God and how they can discern his will. Before they do anything, they must know what is acceptable to him and what they can do to please him. Most issues in the church have to do with their own knowledge, which is limited, imperfect, and often misleading others. For example, in 14:1–23, "the strong" ("those who eat anything") think all food is clean and eat them freely and openly. Their knowledge may be correct from a certain perspective as 1 Cor 8:4–7 says, but it is not right if it leads to harming others. God wants justice and peace in the whole community. Paul's point is: "Knowledge puffs up, but love builds up" (1 Cor 8:1). Likewise, he says in 13:8–10 that love fulfills the law in that God's love must be seen in the love of neighbor. All knowledge or all good things may be useless if there is no love of neighbor in the community.

Therefore, Roman Christians must know what God wants and how they should worship him. God wants their "reasonable or reasoning worship" (*logiken latreia*, 12:1).[1] "Reasonable service" in the NRSV has a connotation that the service or worship must be reasonable. The focus is a thing that must be rational. Thus "reasonable" points to specific actions or things that are considered reasonable. For example, Paul wants his Roman audience to love one another in Christ. But Ian Scott goes one step further and argues that "reasoning worship" is better than "reasonable worship" because the former points to the reasoning mind. That is, the focus is the reasoning process. Scott's view of *logikos* is as follows: It "modifies some human action it consistently distinguishes that act as one either (a) performed by means of reasoned thought or (b) guided by reasoned thought."[2] So Paul wants "his Roman audience to perform a sacrifice that is either offered by engaging in rational ethical deliberation or motivated by rational judgement."[3] So Paul's *logiken latreia* is more than a reasonable service,

---

1. "Reasoning worship" is Ian Scott's term. See Ian Scott, "Your Reasoning Worship," 500–532.

2. Ian Scott, "Your reasoning worship," 525. See also Young's Literal Translation: "your intelligent service."

3. Ian Scott, "Your reasoning worship," 525.

but it must be the service informed by reasoning rooted in Christ. So, "reasoning worship" is certainly better than "spiritual service" Paul does not mean the "spiritual worship" in some modern sense of Christian spirituality or to kind of worship style in tune with spirituality. Rather, *logiken latreia* denotes a holistic service to God that demands the commitment of a whole person.[4] That is why Paul asks Roman Christians "to present their bodies as a living sacrifice, holy and acceptable to God," which is their "reasonable service or worship" (12:1). But their bodies are susceptible to sin because they may be driven their sinful passions. Therefore, what is needed is their dying to sin (c.f., 6:1–23). They have to present their bodies "as a living sacrifice, holy and acceptable to God," which means "by the Spirit to put to death the deeds of the body" (8:13).

In 12:2, Paul talks about the transformation of their minds: "Do not be conformed to this world, but be transformed by the renewing of your minds, so that you may discern what is the will of God—what is good and acceptable and perfect." First, they should not follow "this world," which means they must overcome sin's temptation or their sinful passions that seek their own power at the expense of the weak and marginalized. In this sense, "this world" represents sin's way that does not submit to God and his righteousness. Otherwise, "this world" does not mean an escape from this world. He is not a dualist who thinks this world is an inferior creation by a demiurge. In his view, the world is not itself evil. What is wrong with it is because of sin, which led people to sin against God and his righteousness. The world became a place of chaos and death because of sin. Sin and death spread to all the places. The solution is to live to God by dying to sin, as we explored in Rom 6–7. Therefore, all things, people, institutions, and the empire that do not follow the way of God represents "this world." Thus, he asks them "not to be conformed to this world," but to be transformed by renewing of their minds. That is, they must continue to die to sin and live to God. Renewing of their minds cannot be done once and for all.

12:3-21 MANDATES FOR TRANSFORMATIVE ETHICS

In 12:3–21, Paul gives specific tips to Roman Christians about how they can live as transformed people. They should not think of themselves more highly than they ought to think, but think "with sober judgment, each

---

4. See C. E. B. Cranfield, *A Critical and Exegetical Commentary on the Epistle to the Romans,* Vol. 2, 2.604–5.

according to the measure of faith that God has assigned" (12:3). This means each member of the community is valuable and has a particular role to play for edifying the church. Each one must know what he/she can do best. No one is higher than the others. The measure of faith is assigned by God, which means no one can boast about his/her faith or ignore others. It is God who knows best each person's ability and assigns each the proper work.

They all constitute "one body in Christ," as 12:5 says: "For as in one body we have many members, and not all the members have the same function, so we, who are many, are one body in Christ, and individually we are members one of another." But the question is: What kind of the body is this? Can it be understood primarily as a metaphorical organism that emphasizes unity? From a metaphorical organism perspective, "one body" means one community to which many of its members belong. What is emphasized here is the unity of the community with Christ. That is, Christ is the owner or center of the church. Likewise, "one body in Christ" means one unified community in Christ. But from an alternative perspective, we can read "one body" as an analogy of the body where body parts are connected and work together for the benefits of the whole body. In other words, the body is perceived not as the community but as a body like the human body, which is then understood as a system of solidarity and mutual care. In a social body concept as in a metaphorical organism sense, the human body is understood as a system of hierarchy where not all parts are cared for equally. Such a case is found in the fable of Menenius Agrippa.[5] But in 12:4–5 as well as 1 Cor 12:12–27, Paul's primary concern is not how to maintain the unified community just like a social body in society but how to be one community of mutual caring and mutual support. This is possible by following Christ. So the expression we have in 12:5 is "one body in Christ," which means the community to be informed by Christ. All members work together to help each other and their action is guided by the law of Christ, which means his love of God and the world. They are one not because they have the same thought but because they are connected to Christ-like thinking and behavior. They are members of one another because they understand and

---

5. In this fable, the belly and other body parts are in dispute. The issue is about fairness of life. Other body parts think that life is unfair to them because only they work hard while the belly takes food and eat all the time without work. They tell the belly that they are going to strike against him (the belly). Then the belly says to them: "You can go on strike against me; I will go hungry and die. Then you will have the same fate with me" (This is my paraphrasing of the story). See this fable is retold by Livy, *History of Rome* 2.32.8–12.

help each other. In such a community of love and care with each other, all members rejoice and even suffer together because they are one. This understanding of the body differs from the Stoic metaphor of the body where not all are taken care of equally. Indeed, some elites rejoice at the expense of the weak and the marginalized. Interestingly, in this view, the human body is also understood as hierarchically. For example, the head is more important than other parts. But in a Christ-like community ("Christic body"), there is no hierarchical chain of command; the difference is only the different work by each part. Thus in 12:6–8, Paul says there are "gifts that differ according to the grace given to us: prophecy, in proportion to faith; ministry, in ministering; the teacher, in teaching; the exhorter, in exhortation; the giver, in generosity; the leader, in diligence; the compassionate, in cheerfulness."

After this, Paul gives a long list of exhortations in 12:9–21, which characterizes the Christ-like community's behavior. First, love must be genuine. This means it should not seek one's benefit alone. Rather, it must seek the wellbeing of the whole community ("Love builds up"). Second, evil must be resisted, and what is good must continue. Third, mutual care is needed, and outdoing one another in showing honor is also needed to the Christ-informed, loving community. Fourth, members of the community must be ardent in spirit, which means they must work hard. Fifth, they must "rejoice in hope, be patient in suffering, and persevere in prayer." This means the life in the community is not easy; they must endure hardship while rejoicing at the work of God. Sixth, they must help the poor and strangers. Their love of God must be extended to the most unfortunate. Seventh, they must bless those who persecute them without cursing. This is a hard thing like Jesus's teaching of loving the enemy. Eighth, they must share the joy and sadness of others. This is a life of the human body that all parts feel together because they are connected intimately. Ninth, they must live in harmony with others. The goal of life is not to destroy others or hate them but to promote a life of living together. Tenth, they must be humble and associate with the lowly. This is also a hard thing in Roman society and also in the Christian community in Rome because people flock together based on class or race. Eleventh, they must know their wisdom is very partial or limited. Twelfth, they should not repay anyone evil for evil. This means retaliation is prohibited. Thirteenth, they should never revenge themselves and leave room for the wrath of God. Lastly, they should not be overcome by evil, but overcome evil with good.

13:1-7 DEALING WITH THE GOVERNING AUTHORITIES

12:17–21 is an important ethical basis for Roman Christians' relation to the governing authorities. In these verses, Paul asks Roman churches not to repay evil for evil, but to show good works to all, which means including rulers. He also asks them to live peaceably with all, not to revenge themselves, and to leave room for the wrath of God. Here, peaceable living with "all" must include the Roman government and its leaders. This also means they must recognize their power or authorities because all authorities have been instituted by God (13:1). Paul expresses his thought about the governing authorities in 13:1–2: "Let every person be subject to the governing authorities; for there is no authority except God, and those authorities that exist have been instituted by God. Therefore whoever resists authority resists what God has appointed, and those who resist will incur judgment." Paul's logic here is all powers and authorities belong to God without whom nothing can exist in the world. Therefore, he wants Roman Christians to recognize their authorities and to show good conduct to them. This also means to "pay to all what is due them—taxes to whom taxes are due, revenue to whom revenue is due, respect to whom respect is due, honor to whom honor is due" (13:7). They must do whatever is good to them because "rulers are not a terror to good conduct" (13:3). If Roman Christians do wrong, they should be afraid of them (13:4). Paul warns that the end did not come yet. Until then, they must work hard and cooperate with the government if it is not a terror to them. Otherwise, he worries that they may be considered anti-social or revolutionaries by Rome and that the churches will be in trouble and persecuted. Paul warns that they must work hard until the day of Parousia.

Otherwise, "being subject to the governing authorities" does not mean that Roman churches must support any form of evil acts by Rome and obey Rome in all circumstances. Paul does not seem to say to them to show "blind" obedience to the authorities. On the other hand, Roman authorities or political leaders should not take 13:1 to mean that Christians must submit to them in all circumstances. Paul does not say evil or evil authorities are acceptable to God. Likewise, he does not mean that all authorities are good and just. His thought is not to resist evil by evil or to repay evil for evil. In other words, his strategy is to overcome evil by good (12:21). Paul's thinking is that, even if rulers are evil, violent resistance is not a good one because eventually, God will bring them to justice on the day of wrath, as he said in 2:8–9: "while for those who are self-seeking and who obey not the truth but wickedness, there will be wrath and fury. There will be anguish and distress for everyone who does evil, the Jew first and also the Greek."

13:8-10 LOVE IS THE FULFILLING OF THE LAW

In 13:8-10, Paul expresses his radical view of love: "Owe no one anything, except to love one another; for the one who loves another has fulfilled the law. The commandments, . . . and any other commandment, are summed up in this word, 'Love your neighbor as yourself.' Love does no wrong to a neighbor; therefore, love is the fulfilling of the law." It is very interesting that Paul summarizes the whole law with the single commandment of love of neighbor, while Jesus summarizing with the double commandment of love (Matt 22:34-40). But this does not mean that Paul is more radical than Jesus in ways that he only focuses on the love of neighbor. Paul's point must be the fact that the true love of neighbor evinces the love of God. In other words, the love of God and the love of neighbor are inseparable with each other. Those who love God must love their neighbors. Love is the ultimate virtue that solidifies the wounded community and that heals hurt of people. "Love builds up," while "knowledge puffs up" (1 Cor 8:1). The love of neighbor in 13:8-10 also echoes Gal 5:14: "For the whole law is summed up in a single commandment, 'You shall love your neighbor as yourself.'"[6]

13:11-14 PREPARATION FOR THE LAST DAY

13:11-14 is about the preparation for the last day. As the end is near, Christians must work harder and show good conduct to the world, so that more people would come to God through Christ Jesus. In some sense, not much has changed since they joined a new community of love in Christ because they are still having economic, social hardships due to their faith in the Roman Empire. Nevertheless, they must know what time it is (13:11). Paul reminds them of the coming of the end, exhorting them to live their best. They should not behave like those who do not work or those who just wait

6. Paul's view of love is found in Jesus's teaching in the Sermon on the Mount: "In everything do to others as you would have them do to you; for this is the law and the prophets" (Matt 7:12). The great Rabbi Hillel, a contemporary of Jesus, also taught the radical ethical teaching about the Torah: "What is hateful to you do not do to your neighbor. This is the whole Torah, while the rest is commentary. Go and learn it." Shabbat 31a.

for the Lord all day. They should not live in drunkenness, debauchery, and licentiousness (13:13). Because the day is near, they live honorably in the day, which means showing good works to other people. They must "put on the Lord Jesus," which means to follow his faith and spirit (c.f., 15:1–13).

14:1–23 WELCOMING THOSE WHO ARE WEAK IN FAITH

The Christian community is a community of love and care that has to follow the example of Christ. This means all members have to welcome and accept others who join the community.[7] While all differ from each other and think differently on certain issues such as the Lord's Supper or dietary habits, they are still "one body in Christ," as in 12:4–5. Paul advises Roman churches to "welcome those who are weak in faith" (14:1).[8] These people eat only vegetables because their conscience does not allow for eating meat due to their Jewish customs such as food and dietary laws. Their opinion and lifestyle must be honored. Those who eat anything are strong in faith; their knowledge is correct because "nothing is unclean in itself" (14:14, 20; 1 Cor 8—11). But if there are some weak people struggling to eat meat, the strong people must yield their rights or knowledge and support those weak members. The yielding persons must be those who are strong, not the weak. In fact, as Mark Reasoner argues, the identity of "the strong" includes both Jewish Christians who do not care about Jewish laws and Gentile Christians who have higher social status and feel confident about their Roman

---

7. For more about the Roman church situation, see A. J. M. Wedderburn, *The Reasons for Romans*, 44–65.

8. Philip Esler suggests that in Rome there is inter-house conflict between "Judean" and "non-Judean Christ-followers." The strong are Gentile Christians who eat anything while the weak are Judeans (Esler's preferred term is "Judean" rather than "Jews") who are cautious about what to eat. He also suggests that Paul's letter to the Romans must be read against this conflict situation in which Paul aims to establish a new common group identity in Christ. This reading of Esler makes a better sense than Mark Nanos's reading that the "weak" are non-Christian Jews and that the "strong" are both Jewish and Gentile followers of Jesus. On the other hand, Mark Reasoner suggests that the use of "the strong" and "the weak" in Rom 14:1–15:13 should be understood more broadly in Roman context and beyond a simple division between ethnicities: for example, Gentile Christians and Jewish Christians. That is, "the strong" includes some Jewish Christians who are free from Mosaic Law, while "the weak" includes some Gentile Christians who are very sensitive to Jewish laws (perhaps, they are former God-fearers). Moreover, "the strong" also includes some Gentile Christians who are confident about their Roman culture. See Philip Esler, *Conflict and Identity in Romans*, 339–356. See Mark Nanos, *The Mystery of Romans*, 85–165. See also Mark Reasoner, *The Strong and the Weak*, 202–218.

culture.[9] All these "strong" people must yield their power and rights to "the weak" who are marginalized in society. The important ethical rule in the community is not the absolute knowledge, power, or social status but mutual care with one another.

Therefore, the strong should not judge those who are weak in faith (14:3–4). If they do so, they stand against them, making them fall (14:4). Moreover, Paul says in 1 Cor 1:26–28 that God cares for the nobodies: "God chose what is foolish in the world to shame the wise; God chose what is weak in the world to shame the strong; God chose what is low and despised in the world, things that are not, to reduce to nothing things that are."[10] Therefore, all must act "in honor of the Lord" who loved those who are weak (14:6–7). Paul says in 14:7–8: "We do not live to ourselves, and we do not die to ourselves. If we live, we live to the Lord, and if we die, we die to the Lord; so then, whether we live or whether we die, we are the Lord's." Therefore no one can pass judgment on others in the community (14:9–13). If they do so, they are against the Lord who died for the weak. The issue is not over whose view is right or correct but over their judgment and despisement of others. Paul warns that "we will all stand before the judgment seat of God" (14:10). Eventually, each "will be accountable to God" (14:12). To avoid the judgment, what is needed is an ethical sensitivity to those who are weak in faith. Thus, Paul says: "So do not let your good be spoken of as evil" (14:16).

Paul also talks about the desirable community ethics, alluding to "the kingdom of God" (*basileia tou theou*), which means "the rule, reign, or activity of God," not a place or a time in the future. Thus, he says: "For the kingdom of God is not food and drink but righteousness and peace and joy in the Holy Spirit" (14:17). In other words, the beloved community of God in Christ must seek "righteousness and peace and joy in the Holy Spirit." Readers are reminded of Paul's earlier saying in 8:14: "For all who are led by the Spirit of God are children of God." To become children of God, they are to be led by the Spirit, which means putting to death the deeds of the body (8:13). As God's people, they must show good works to the world and pursue peace and mutual building (14:19). Everything must be done from faith (14:22–23). This faith is none other than trusting God, being led by the Spirit, and following Christ. So Paul says: "For whatever does not

9. Mark Reasoner, *The Strong and the Weak*, 202–218.

10. See Alain Badiou, *Saint Paul*, 86–106.

proceed from faith is sin" (14:23). Sin is not to respect others. There is no God with that person who ignores others.

15:1-13 FOLLOWING THE WAY OF CHRIST

In 15:1–13, Paul addresses the strong and asks them to "put up with the failings of the weak." He gives an example of Christ to them (15:3). Christ did not please himself, advocating for the rule of God. More than that, he "has become a servant (*diakonos*) of the circumcised on behalf of the truth of God in order that he might confirm the promises given to the patriarchs, and in order that the Gentiles might glorify God for his mercy" (15:8–9). This means that Jesus was faithful to God and testified to the truth of God. He did not overthrow the law or Abraham's covenant. Rather, "Christ is the fulfillment (*telos*) of the law so that there may be righteousness for everyone who has faith" (10:4). Jesus proclaimed the good news of God and disclosed God's righteousness through faithfulness. The gospel spreads to all because of him and through him. Likewise, the strong should not please themselves but should please their neighbor "for the purpose of building up the neighbor" (15:2). He also encourages them to stay in hope by following "the God of steadfastness and encouragement" and "to live in harmony with one another, in accordance with Christ Jesus" (15:5).

SECTION IV

15:14–16:27
Concluding Matters

HAVING DEALT WITH THE essence of the gospel (Rom 1–11) and the gospel's power of transformation in the community and society (12–15:13), Paul moves to his last topic, which was hinted in 1:14–15: "I am a debtor both to Greeks and to barbarians, both to the wise and to the foolish— hence my eagerness to proclaim the gospel to you also who are in Rome." He is eager to visit Rome and go to Spain to proclaim the gospel of God and of Christ. Since he feels that he covered most regions in his proclamation of the gospel, he plans to make the last journey to Spain. In his view, Spain is considered not only the end of the earth but the most barbarous country where many have not heard the gospel at all. In 15:14–24, he makes a case that he must go there through the support of Roman churches. In 15:25–33, he mentions about his trip to Jerusalem to deliver the collection for the poor at Jerusalem and asks Roman Christians to pray for him, so that he may be safe from the threat of the unbelieving Jews in Judea. Again, here, he reminds them of his determined journey to Spain. Then Rom16 concludes the letter and greets many individuals in Rome.

Outline of 15:14–33

15:14–24 Paul's desire to proclaim the gospel in Spain
15:25–33 Delivering the collection to the poor saints in Jerusalem
16:1–27 Conclusion

15:14–24 PAUL'S DESIRE TO PROCLAIM THE GOSPEL IN SPAIN

In 15:14, Paul commends Roman Christians' good character, all knowledge, and their teaching. But he does not explore more about these good things. Instead, he reminds them of what he has written in the letter. That is, he tells them that he became "a minister of Christ Jesus to the Gentiles in the priestly service of the gospel of God, so that the offering of the Gentiles may be acceptable, sanctified by the Holy Spirit" (15:16). As an apostle to the Gentiles, his job is to proclaim "the gospel of God" through "the gospel of Christ." The gospel of God is for what he was called and set apart (1:1), and its content is God's righteousness— understood as his steadfast love and justice. Now God's righteousness has been disclosed through Christ's faithfulness (3:21–22), which constitutes "the gospel of Christ." Then, God justifies the one who shares the faithfulness of Christ (3:26). He is not ashamed of the gospel because "it is the power of God for salvation to everyone who has faith, to the Jew first and also to the Greek" (1:16). "The righteous one will live by faith" (1:17). Paul's gospel is all about this above. He also proclaims the gospel of God through Christ. Otherwise, he does not preach his own message about God or Christ. His gospel is anyone can be hopeful in God through faith. All are invited to the love of God and to the faithfulness of Jesus Christ, his Son. His job is to bring Gentiles to God. In particular, he wants to go to Spain to proclaim the gospel there, thinking he covered all mission areas from Jerusalem and as far as Illyricum. This does not mean he covered literally all places in those regions. He means that most important cities were covered by him and other Christian missionaries. Also, there are already lively Christian churches and activities. Therefore, he has the ambition to proclaim the gospel to new people or place that has never heard Christ's name (15:20–21). This new place is Spain (15:24). He desires to go there via Rome after he has fellowship with and support from Roman churches (15:23–24).

15:25–33 DELIVERING THE COLLECTION TO THE POOR AT JERUSALEM

Paul's collection efforts to help the poor at Jerusalem is outstanding. Macedonia and Achaia helped him to collect enough resources, and now he is en route to Jerusalem to deliver them. But he could have delivered them later after his visit to Rome and having a mission in Spain. But he wanted to take care of this delivery project first. In some sense, it is hard to understand why this delivery is the priority for him because his mission to Spain is urgent (c.f., 1:11, 14–15). But his priority is understandable in view of his mission strategy. That is, he does not want others (especially, Jews and Jewish Christians) to misunderstand him. In other words, if he goes to Jerusalem, he wants to make sure that he is not a betrayer of Judaism and that he cares for his own people. Moreover, as he explored in Rom 11, he wants to tell Jews that his gospel does not need to reject Israel or God's covenant with them. Moreover, the Gentiles' material support can be considered a gift to the spiritual blessings of Jews (12:27; c.f., 2 Cor 8:13–15). All this above taken together, Paul's priority to deliver the collection for the poor at Jerusalem goes beyond a matter of charity. After a successful delivery, he plans a trip to Spain via Rome, as he says: "So, when I have completed this, and have delivered to them what has been collected, I will set out by way of you to Spain" (15:28). But he is uncertain about his safety because there may be a threat of "the unbelievers in Judea" (15:31). So he asks Roman Christians to pray for him so that his "ministry to Jerusalem may be acceptable to the saints" (15:31). If he makes a success in Jerusalem, he would come to Rome and have fellowship with Roman Christians, preparing for a historical journey to Spain. Then, he blesses them: "The God of peace be with all of you. Amen" (15:33).

16:1–27 CONCLUSION

Rom 16 contains matters of letter ending as follows: letter-bearer, Phoebe (16:1–2); twenty-six individuals greeted by Paul (16:3–16); Paul's warning and concerns (16:17–20); greetings from his associates (16:21–24); and doxology (16:25–27).

Phoebe is Paul's co-worker and she is a deacon (*diakonos*) of the church at Cenchreae northeast of Corinth. *Diakonos* (the masculine noun) is a leader or minister at a local church. There is not yet a church office called *diakonos*. In Paul's congregations, women are active workers in the church, receiving the gifts of the Spirit equally with men (1 Cor 12–14). Some are leaders of the church: for example, Phoebe, Prisca, and Junia. Phoebe was also a benefactor or patron (*prostatis*), who helped the church and Paul's ministry financially (16:2–3). Paul commends her as a carrier of his letter.

In 16:3–5, he greets Prisca and Aquila, a Jewish couple who supported Paul when they were in Corinth (1 Cor 16:19). The other notable Jewish couple is Andronicus and Junia who are called "prominent apostles."[1] Junia is Andronicus's wife who is also prominent among the apostles. Later churches did not like this idea that a woman is called "apostle." All of sudden, Junia was changed to Junias (male name). The list of greeted individuals continues until Rom 16:16. Regarding the question of how Paul came to know and greet all these individuals if he did not make a visit to Rome before, one plausible answer is Paul may have met them during Claudius's expulsion of Jews from Rome in about mid-40s.

In 16:17, Paul is concerned about "those who cause dissensions and offenses, in opposition to the teaching that you have learned" and asks Roman Christians to avoid them. God's mercy does not mean to tolerate those offenders in regards to the gospel's character and purpose. "To avoid them" means not to follow them or associate with them. They do not serve the Lord, "but their own appetites" (16:18). They also "deceive the hearts of the simple-minded by smooth talk and flattery" (16:18). Therefore, their behavior betrays the gospel and ruins the community.

In 16:21–23, there are Paul's associates who also greet the same individuals: notable are Timothy (Paul's co-worker), Tertius (the writer of this letter), Gaius (host to Paul's church), and Erastus (the city treasurer). Then a doxology follows in 16:25–27. Here again, he refers to his gospel that is the power of God through the proclamation of Jesus Christ. Now is the time that all the Gentiles come to God through faith. This final "Amen" is the end of the letter. In the end, we do not know whether he made his journey to Spain. But his passion to share the gospel of God through Christ Jesus remained effective to many to this day. So it was a success.

---

1. Eldon Jay Epp, *Junia*, 23–81.

Bibliography

Abelard, Peter. *Commentary on the Epistle to the Romans*, trans. Stephen R. Cartwright. Washington, DC: Catholic University Press of America, 2011.

Aulén, Gustaf. *Christus Victor: A Historical Study of the Three Main Types of the Idea of the Atonement*, trans. A. G. Hebert. London: SPCK, 1945.

Achtemeier, Paul. *Romans*. Interpretation. Atlanta, GA: John Knox, 1985.

Badiou, Alain. *Saint Paul: The Foundation of Universalism*, trans. Ray Brassier. Stanford, CA: Stanford University Press, 2003.

Bailey, Daniel. *Jesus as the Mercy Seat: the semantics and theology of Paul's use of Hilasterion in Romans 3:25*. Doctoral thesis, University of Cambridge, 1999.

Bassler, Jouette. *Navigating Paul: An Introduction to Key Theological Concepts*. Louisville, KY: Westminster John Knox, 2007.

Bauer, Walter and Frederick Danker, eds. *Greek-English Lexicon of the New Testament and Other Early Christian Literature*. Chicago, IL: University of Chicago Press, 2000.

Bird, Michael. *The Saving Righteousness of God*. Waynesboro, GA: Paternoster, 2007.

Boswell, John. *Christianity, Social Tolerance, and Homosexuality: Gay People in Western Europe from the Beginning of the Christian Era to the Fourteenth Century*. Chicago, IL: The University of Chicago Press, 1980.

Brondos, David. *Paul on the Cross: Reconstructing the Apostle's Story of Redemption*. Minneapolis: Fortress, 2006.

Brown, M. J. "Paul's Use of *doulos christou Iesou* in Romans 1:1." *JBL* (2001) 120:723–37.

Brownson, James. *Bible, Gender, Sexuality: Reframing the Church's Debate on Same-Sex Relationships*. Grand Rapids, MI: Eerdmans, 2013.

Bryant, K. Edwin. *Paul and the Rise of the Slave: Death and Resurrection of the Oppressed in the Epistle to the Romans*. Boston, MA: Brill, 2016.

Bultmann, Rudolf. "pisteuo ktl," *TDNT* 6 (1968) 219–20.

Byrne, Brendan. *Galatians and Romans*. Collegeville, MN: Liturgical Press, 2010.

Cousar, Charles B. *A Theology of the Cross: The Death of Jesus in the Pauline Letters*. Minneapolis: Fortress, 1990.

Cranfield, C. E. B. *A Critical and Exegetical Commentary on the Epistle to the Romans*, Vol. 1–2. Edinburgh: T & T Clark, 2004.

Davies, Glenn. *Faith and Obedience in Romans: A Study in Romans 1–4*. Sheffield: Sheffield Academic Press, 1990.

Dodd, C. H. *The Epistle of Paul to the Romans*. London: Collins, 1959.

———. *The Bible and the Greeks*. London: Hodder & Stoughton, 1964.

Dowd, Sharyn and Elizabeth Struthers Malbon. "The Significance of Jesus' Death in Mark: Narrative Context and Authorial Audience." *Journal of Biblical Literature* 125.2 (2006): 271–297.

Dunn, James. *Romans 1—8*. Dallas, TX: Word Books, 1988.

———. *The New Perspective on Paul: Revised Edition*. Grand Rapids, MI: Eerdmans, 2008.

Epp, Eldon Jay. *Junia: The First Woman Apostle*. Minneapolis: Fortress, 2005.

Esler, Philip F. *Conflict and Identity in Romans: The Social Setting of Paul's Letter*. Minneapolis: Fortress, 2003.

Fitzmyer, Joseph. *Romans*. New Haven, CT: Yale Univ. Press, 1993.

Fredrickson, David. "Natural and Unnatural Use in Romans 1:24–27: Paul and the Philosophic Critique of Eros." In *Homosexuality, Science, and the 'Plain Sense' of Scripture*," edited by David L. Balch, 197–222. Grand Rapids, MI: Eerdmans, 2000.

Grieb, Katherine. *The Story of Romans: A Narrative Defense of God's Righteousness*. Louisville, KY: WJKP, 2002.

Haacker, Klaus. *The Theology of Paul's Letter to the Romans*. Cambridge: Cambridge University Press, 2003.

Hamerton-Kelly, Robert. *Sacred Violence: Paul's Hermeneutic of the Cross*.Minneapolis: Fortress, 1992.

Hays, Richard. *The Faith of Jesus Christ: The Narrative Substructure of Galatians 3:1–4:11*. Grand Rapids, MI: Eerdmans, 2002.

Jewett, Robert. *Romans: A Commentary*. Minneapolis, MN: Fortress, 2007.

Johnson, Adam. ed. *T&T Clark Companion to Atonement*. New York: T&T Clark, 2017.

Johnson, Luke Timothy. *Reading Romans: A Literary and Theological Commentary*. Macon, GA: Smyth & Helwys, 1999.

———. "Life-Giving Spirit: The Ontological Implications of Resurrection." *Stone-Campbell Journal*, 15.1 (2012): 75–89.

———. "Rom 3:21–26 and the faith of Jesus." *Catholic Biblical Quarterly*, 44.1 (1982): 77–90.

Käsemann, Ernst. Trans. W. J. Montague. *New Testament Questions of Today*. Philadelphia, PA: SCM-Canterbury Press, 1969.

———. *Commentary on Romans*, trans. Geoffrey Bromiley. Eerdmans, 1980.

Keck, Leander. *Romans*. Nashville, TN: Abingdon, 2005.

Keener, Craig S. *Romans: A New Covenant Commentary*. Eugene, OR: Cascade, 2009.

Kim, Yung Suk. *A Theological Introduction to Paul's Letters: Exploring a Threefold Theology of Paul*. Eugene, OR: Cascade, 2011.

Kirby, J. T. "The Syntax of Romans 5:12: A Rhetorical Approach." *NTS* 33 (1987): 283–86.

Leenhardt, Franz. *The Epistle of Saint Paul to the Romans: A Commentary*. Trans. H. Knight. London: Lutterworth, 1961.

Longenecker, Bruce. "Pistis in Romans 3:25: Neglected Evidence for the Faithfulness of Christ." *New Testament Studies* 39 (1993) 478–480.

Longenecker, Richard. *Introducing Romans: Critical Concerns in Paul's Most Famous Letter*. Grand Rapids: Eerdmans, 2011.

———. *The Epistle to the Romans*. Grand Rapids, MI: Eerdmans, 2016.

Martin, Dale. *Sex and the Single Savior: Gender and Sexuality in Biblical Interpretation*. Louisville, KY: W/JKP, 2006.

Matera, Frank. "Reconciliation." Harper's Bible Dictionary, ed. P.J. Achtemeier et al., 856. New York, NY: Harper Collins, 1985.

Macgregor, G. H. C. "The Concept of the Wrath of God in the New Testament." *NTS* 7 (1960–61) 101–9.

Michel, Otto. *Der Briefe an die Römer*. Göttingen: Vandenhoeck & Ruprecht, 1978.

Moule, C. F. D. "Punishment and Retribution: An Attempt to Delimit Their Scope in New Testament Thought." *Svensk Exegetisk Arsbok* 30 (1966) 21–36.

Murray, John. *The Epistle to the Romans: The English Text with Introduction, Exposition, and Notes*. Grand Rapids: Eerdmans, 1997.

Nanos, Mark. *The Mystery of Romans: The Jewish Context for Paul's Letter*. Minneapolis: Fortress, 1996.

Powers, Daniel. *Salvation through Participation: An Examination of the Notion of the Believers' Corporate Unity with Christ in Early Christian Soteriology*. Leuven: Peeters, 2001.

Reasoner, Mark. *The Strong and the Weak: Romans 14:1–15:13 in Context*. Cambridge: Cambridge University Press, 1999.

———. *Romans in Full Circle: A History of Interpretation*. Louisville, KY: Westminster John Knox, 2005

Sanders, E. P. *Paul and Palestinian Judaism: A Comparison of Patterns of Religion*. Philadelphia, PA: Fortress, 1977.

———. "Covenantal Nomism Revisited," *Jewish Studies Quarterly* 16, no. 1 (2009): 23–55.

Scott, Ian. "'Your Reasoning Worship': ΛΟΓΙΚΟΣ in Romans 12:1 and Paul's Ethics of Rational Deliberation," *The Journal of Theological Studies* 69.2 (2018) 500–532.

Scroggs, Robin. *New Testament and Homosexuality*. Minneapolis, MN: Fortress, 1983.

Scullion, John. "Righteousness (OT)." *Anchor Bible Dictionary* 5 (1992) 735.

Stendahl, Krister. *Final Account: Paul's Letter to the Romans*. Minneapolis, MN: Fortress, 1995.

Stowers, Stanley K. *A Rereading of Romans: Justice, Jews, and Gentiles*. New Haven: Yale University Press, 1995.

Stuhlmacher, Peter. *Reconciliation, Law, & Righteousness: Essays in Biblical Theology*. Philadelphia, PA: Fortress, 1987.

Talbert, Charles H. *Romans*. Macon, GA: Smyth and Helwys, 2002.

Tannehill, Robert. *Dying and Rising with Christ: A Study in Pauline Theology*. Berlin: Töpelmann, 1967.

Tasker, R. V. G. *The Biblical Doctrine of the Wrath of God*. London: Tyndale, 1951.

Wasserman, Emma. *The Death of the Soul in Romans 7: Sin, Death, and the Law in Light of Hellenistic Moral Psychology*. WUNT 2/256. Tübingen: Mohr Siebeck, 2008.

Wedderburn, A. J. M. *The Reasons for Romans*. Minneapolis: Fortress, 1991.